T0121504

The Unboxing

A Black Girl's Journey of
Mental Health, Faith, and Identity

Nicole E. Williams

WESTBOW
PRESS®
A DIVISION OF THOMAS NELSON
& ZONDERVAN

WestBow Press books may be ordered through booksellers or by contacting:

WestBow Press
A Division of Thomas Nelson & Zondervan
1663 Liberty Drive
Bloomington, IN 47403
www.westbowpress.com
844-714-3454

ISBN: 978-1-9736-7175-6 (sc)
ISBN: 978-1-9736-7174-9 (e)

Print information available on the last page.

WestBow Press rev. date: 6/28/2022

Dedication

To my siblings, Sarah, Hannah, and Wil—God has
great plans for you; don't let this world distract you.

To my cousin Zoe and all young girls who know there is
more to life than what they are currently experiencing.

To my parents, Teresa and Sidney—you keep serving despite
everything that tells you there is no hope. Thank you for
dedicating your life to freeing people from their chains.

To my future children—I know being a teenager is hard,
but God can use you as soon as you let Him. You don't
have to wait for adulthood to "figure it all out."

Foreword

Nicole, I am honored to write the foreword for your first book. Each page reminded me of the moment I found out my first child would be a little girl. My life and my heart began a new journey when you were conceived. I still remember like it was yesterday when I heard your first heartbeat. From that day until your birth, every day was filled with anticipation. Your mom and I wanted everything to be better than our childhood experiences. We wanted to shield you from all spiritual, emotional, and physical harm. Yet, we knew this was beyond our ability. We were both still healing from our childhood and trying to discern what it meant to be married with children.

From the first time I held you in my arms, you looked at me like I could do no wrong with your eyes that made the world disappear around us. I never felt a connection like that with anyone. No words can fully grasp all the emotions I felt at that moment. On the one hand, I was overwhelmed and unprepared for such a great responsibility and yet, on the other hand, fully committed to becoming the best father I could be. I can't remember our connection's first change, but I could feel the difference. We couldn't find the language to communicate what was happening. This was an unfamiliar experience based on the lack of emotional intimacy in my upbringing.

Reading the pages of your book was difficult for me, yet every sentence peeled away layers of uncertainty, drawing me closer still. Your willingness to explore painful moments in your life and to give words to what you could not explain in the past will encourage others.

Too many children live in silence and cannot articulate their feelings. Your academic achievement and spiritual maturity are evident in how you convey your narrative. You not only reveal the painful and complex realities of being a teenager but also share a pathway of hope and healing.

Thank you for trusting me with your secrets and allowing me to experience your truth. You have the most amazing heart; please never lose that. Regardless of the path you choose in this life, you will always be my victorious princess.

Love,
Dad

Preface

I am seated in a village cafe in a Muslim country that only 30 Americans have ever visited before me. The people around me are watching me intently, seemingly fascinated by my presence. I cling to my journal, and I write as a means of escape and a way to understand what I am experiencing. Here, my name is Diari Mballo. Diari Mballo knows that she is a Black woman—there is no hiding that, but Diari Mballo has always wanted to be white. Diari Mballo has always desired acceptance. She has spent most of her life looking for approval from her dad, school, community, and men—anywhere she could get it. She doesn't know who she is in all this striving. When she looks in the mirror, she does not know the girl who stares back at her. She is afraid she might never find acceptance. She is saddened. She thought the acceptance she was looking for would finally meet her in the motherland of Africa—the place from which her ancestors were stripped centuries ago—but even there, she struggles to find it. Diari looks back up at the people around her. Her skin is like theirs, but she knows her mind is not. She remembers that she is American and feels a deep sadness—she does not belong here, and she knows it.

At 11 am, she gathers with her six other peers and two instructors for a morning check-in. She is surrounded by three white Americans and four other individuals from Mexico, Colombia, Wales, and Senegal, respectively. She is saddened because she does not belong. She loves that her group is diverse—a pleasant change from her predominantly white high school, but she grieves because she longs for someone to understand her experiences. She longs for a community where she can belong.

As much as she wishes to be, Diari knows she is not Diari Mballo. She knows that this fantasy of Senegalese life will eventually end, and she must face the realities of her true identity: Nicole Williams. Nicole Williams is a Black American, church-going girl with self-hatred, insecurity, and suppressed emotions. She doesn't want to claim any of these traits at her core. She does not know what to do with herself. She does not understand herself. She wishes she could forever remain known as Diarri Mballo or Fatou Diagne, or any of the other names she would receive during the year she spent living in Senegal. But she must return to America as Nicole Williams, and learn to live and love as Nicole, a task that would require immense time, much emotional labor, and an endless amount of divine intervention.

———◆———

We are all on the search for acceptance and love. Through no fault of our own, we search for these things in the ways that society has suggested we should. Some of us use academics; others use Instagram. We put masks on and do things to distract people from seeing the real us. The us that is hurting, the us that is vulnerable, the us that desperately desires acceptance and love. In this age of Instagram models, we are forced to pretend that we are okay when, in reality, we are not. We are constantly trying to juggle life and our own inner battles. Beyoncé confidently asserts "I woke up like this," but most of us hate the way we look when we wake up in the morning—we think we need to cover ourselves up with makeup or the "right" friends. Incessant advertisements make us feel like we need things that we really don't in order to have worth. *If I have these Adidas, if I wear these brands, if I buy this makeup, then finally I will be accepted.* Many of us are driven by our need for others' approval. We unknowingly trade authenticity for conformity at the expense of our own happiness. Many of us sing Cardi B's "Best Life" and other carefree anthems, yet spend hours thinking about what to post on Instagram next or what someone else is thinking about us. If we're honest, we know that we often spend more time thinking about what others expect from us than considering what we want. We often say "I'm livin' my best life" at parties with friends in the high moments, but have no real vision for our future. We each have a story and a unique voice, but we often miss the beauty of our own authenticity because we want so badly to fit in.

Friend after friend has shared with me how the stress of school has led them into a deep depression, panic attacks, and even serious thoughts of suicide. Instead of confronting the deep-seated issues that lie at the root of these symptoms, they sweep them under the rug to go back to the demands of daily life. While we live in a culture that claims this is okay, it is not. It is not okay to suppress our most innate desire to live authentically and be loved fully. I see too many people in my generation either settling for what they think they have to be based on others' perceptions, limiting themselves because of their pasts, or a detrimental combination of the two. The complacency, passivity, and pain that we now live in are so far from the fulfilling and joyful life that God created us to live.

Contrary to what culture dictates, we can live free from the need for masks and other people's approval. What if I told you you didn't need the makeup, those friends, or other things to make you worthy of love? There is so much more to life than settling, and that is the essential message I want you to take away from reading this book. I am so convinced that there is a "better life" available to us, that I am willing to be completely transparent about my own life so that you can tap into greater freedom. For years, I wore all the masks. I worked to have the perfect Instagram feed so my life would look flawless. I even photoshopped my own body to look slimmer than I was. I let my performance in school become a key determinant of my sense of self-worth. It pains me to see so many of my peers live a life in which they constantly feel they have something to prove because I have been there and now see there is a way out.

In order to live our best lives, we must take active steps to unpack who we really are and to pull away from who we are not. We must learn to do this with God's guidance. It is only the Holy Spirit that can lead us on this journey. We must reclaim the power we've given to culture, society, and other people to tell us who we are, and place it back into God's hands. We must surrender our lives to God and ask Him to reveal the vision of His heart for our lives. We must work to connect deeply with who we are in Christ and ask Him to show us how to live. We must learn to address our fears and ask for the courage to persevere in life in spite of them. We must choose to unconditionally accept and love ourselves as creations of God. This starts with knowing how deeply we are loved and accepted by God. Knowing His love allows us to break free from the need for others' approval and from the labels of victim and failure we accept for ourselves. When we choose to be the most authentic version of ourselves that God created us to be, we begin to tear at the very fabric of our culture—one that is built off the manipulation of our insecurities and our need for significance.

While this is the ultimate life that each of us has the potential to live, it is not so easy to get there. It requires a process that I call "unboxing." Doing the inner work today will make us the leaders of our generations. One of the first and most difficult steps of unboxing is becoming aware of our conditioning. It is critical to recognize that the very nature of our conditioning is silent, subtle, and almost invisible. It is natural that we are not conscious of it, but it is there in our subconscious thoughts and actions. All of us have been conditioned by our environment. Everything that we believe and the ways we operate originated from an experience we had with someone or something outside of ourselves. We do not act independently of the world. We can believe that we are independent and that we make decisions based solely on our own dreams and desires, but we often don't. Only God can make us aware of our conditioning. As we come to understand what external factors and experiences impact us, God empowers us to use that knowledge for charting the paths we truly desire to take.

The process of unboxing requires that we reflect on:

- The way we were raised
- Experiences that initiated cycles in our lives
- The context in which we are living
- Philosophies that influence our thinking
- Limiting beliefs
- Fears and insecurities

Our ability to become our truest ourselves is dependent on our courage to allow God to shed light on these critical aspects of our lives. It is when we become aware of these influences, that we truly begin living "our best life," a life full of vision and purpose that God has set out for us.

I started writing this book just after finishing high school as I was searching for a way to become my most authentic self. I continued writing it near the end of my gap year when I had just gone through so much unboxing but still had so much more to process and unlearn. I finally finished the book my freshman year of college as I became more settled in my identity, started going to therapy, and began prioritizing my mental, emotional, and spiritual health more. This story is full of revelation God blessed me to gain through each of those transformative parts of my journey. This story is full of revelation God blessed me to gain through each of those transformative parts of my journey.

This journey will look different for everyone. The journey that I share will likely be radically different from yours because each of us has unique gifts, challenges, and experiences. My hope in publishing this book is that my story can aid you in forging your own path of authentic living. It was others sharing their testimonies that made the difference for me in my walk, so I pray that I can just be one more voice pushing you in the right direction for yours.

Join me as I share my journey of unlearning all the things I thought I had to do to be accepted and learning to live my most free unapologetic life. I am hopeful that as you read the steps I took on my path to freedom, you will continue to progress on your own as well.

Acknowledgments

Thank you to my grandparents, for loving
and supporting me unconditionally.

I am eternally grateful for Pastor Michael Todd and
Transformation Church in Tulsa, Oklahoma, your
ministry has fed into my life indescribably.

I am thankful for the ministry of Lauryn Hill,
whose MTV Unplugged Album gave me the courage
to keep writing when I felt like giving up.

Thank you to the International Baptist Church in Dakar, Senegal
for being my church home during the first year of my unboxing.

Last, but not least, thank you, God, my Father and Friend,
the Author and Finisher of my faith, and the One who put
it on my heart to write this book. Thank you for giving me
a story to tell and gracing me to tell it, for your glory.

Contents

Introduction

Sitting in my best friend's mom's car on the way to a social activism event at a nearby high school, I would receive the news that would direct the next four years of my life. On "Ivy Day," March 30th at 5 pm., I would hear back from Harvard, Yale, Princeton, Columbia, University of Pennsylvania, and Dartmouth. Even before this fateful day, however, I had received full rides to Kenyon College, Williams College, Wellesley College, Howard University, Vassar College, George Washington University, and Bowdoin University, but this was the *real* moment. Make or break. If I had made it into even one of the Ivies then I knew I would *really* be successful, and that all of my hard work would have been worth it. With my friend Bella in the passenger's seat, her mom driving, and her younger sister next to me in the back, I began to open my online decision letters from the Ivies.

Brown was the first one I opened. This was the school I applied Early Decision to and originally was deferred (aka moved to the regular decision pool). It was my top choice.

"It is with **great regret…**" Denied.

Next, Columbia… "… chosen to **postpone…**" Waitlisted.

Dartmouth… "**denied…**"

UPenn… "It is with genuine **regret….**"

Harvard, my middle school dream… "I am very **sorry …**"

Yale… "I am **genuinely sorry…**"

At this point, I had all but given up. I signed onto my Princeton account, bracing myself for another "genuine" rejection.

Princeton... "CONGRATULATIONS!"

"I can't believe it!" That was all I could manage to say for the next five minutes during that car ride. I couldn't believe I had done it. I, Nicole Elizabeth Williams, with a 29 ACT score, was accepted into an Ivy League University. I made it! I had succeeded! Surely, there was nothing else to strive for. I sat in that car ride, literally incapable of wiping the smile off of my face. I smiled so much, for so long that my cheek muscles began twitching.

"I am so proud, Colie! I knew you would get in! See, Brown doesn't deserve you." Bella exclaimed.

"We are so proud of you!" Bella's mom exclaimed. As they continued to praise my hard work and success, I immediately texted my parents. They were thrilled! With all the important people in my life proud of me, I myself extremely proud of my work—I felt, at that moment, that nothing could be better, and I would never desire anything again.

But of course, the voice that I knew all too well, began to speak to me.

"You didn't get into Brown and they have a higher acceptance rate than Princeton. What is wrong with you? I told you, you shouldn't have gotten that B+ in AP English Language. And, you didn't get into Harvard? You should have done better in high school. You really couldn't manage to get into *two* Ivies? Only one? Really?" The unidentified, and yet all too familiar self-deprecating voice in my mind would not leave me alone.

"I got into Princeton! It's like the best school in the country, why does that matter?" I tried to plead with it, rationalize with it, but it wouldn't budge.

"You could have done better. Most people who get into Princeton also get into other Ivies, too. You aren't as good as them." I suddenly began to feel sad and empty—feelings I knew all too well. My seven-year dream of Ivy League success—was a failure. "You never should have tried," the voice continued. That night I went through extremes of being joyful about the acceptance and feeling incredibly inadequate.

As the days continued and more people found out about my Princeton acceptance, I was met with an increasing number of "congratulations," "we are so proud," and "I knew you would get in!" When I was around people who were praising me, I felt good. When I was alone, my self-deprecating thoughts would kill any of my attempts to feel proud of myself. As the days turned into weeks, the emptiness and defeat I felt only grew, but I would just try and distract myself with school work. The Princeton acceptance gave way to trying to figure out how I would plan for graduate school. I lost the joy of the process, and became consumed by the next hoops to jump through in life—none of which were bringing me joy. Even though my insecurity, self-hatred, and isolation were stealing my joy, I still maintained facades of perfection because I wanted to feel significant.

One day, when my entire grade was in the auditorium, my principal came up to me in front of all three hundred of my peers and hugged me. "I am so proud of you!" "It's no big deal," I thought to myself. Other students in my high school got into Ivies, and some of them got into *more than one* Ivy. I would never say it out loud, but there was a small part of me that thought, "I'm not as good as they are."

"Thank you!" I managed to respond, but internally it was as if I couldn't help but take each compliment and follow it up with a self-deprecating thought. This was supposed to be it, and yet I felt myself already preparing for life's next obstacles—internships, graduate school, a career. The thought of all of that work didn't inspire me for the future, it drained me.

The joy over my acceptance only lasted for a short period of time. The emptiness I felt before the acceptance remained. I looked at my body, seventy pounds overweight; I never exercised; I had a habit of overeating, emotionally eating, and binge eating. I was extremely disappointed with how I had abused my body for so long. In all of my attempts to feel whole, I still felt empty. In all of my efforts to find significance, even after the Princeton acceptance, I found myself just as insecure as my 12-year-old middle school self.

What was it that *I* wanted? Who did *I* aspire to be? I never asked myself these questions. I was always outward-looking, not because I was selfless, but because I didn't like myself. All that I could see was the striving required to maintain facades in my community and the insecurity that I was left with when I went home. I couldn't enjoy the beauty that was my life. Instead, I spent time trying to maintain facades. I was so focused on my academic goals, my perception of other people's expectations of me, and my own self-hatred that I didn't take the time to think about how my life events and mindsets were negatively impacting my ability to make healthy decisions that I could truly be at peace with.

In the last two years of high school, I developed an eye twitch that would come at times of great stress and sleep deprivation. After high school graduation, when I was supposed to be relaxing, the slightest stressful situation would cause my eye to twitch. No matter how much I slept, I always felt tired. The thought of brushing my teeth made me exhausted. I was tired of being tired. I began to wonder about the greater, unseen forces at play in my life. I didn't have any obligations from school anymore, yet I still felt like a slave, but to what? What was weighing me down? Why didn't I feel free to have fun, to do what I want?

"Why?" I pleaded to God one night, "Why do I feel so empty?

Is this all you have for me? Is this it? Is this what life is supposed to be? A series of hoops to jump through? I'm a Christian, for crying out loud. I have done everything right. Why do I feel so empty?" At the peak of this depression, I began to wonder—how is it that someone accepted to Princeton could still feel extremely insecure and unworthy? After all, was it not the "cream of the crop" that went to Ivy League schools? There was so much that didn't feel creamy before or after the acceptance. In fact, I nearly felt worse about myself after the acceptance. But I still wondered again: is it that maybe this emptiness is just a trigger of a greater emotional and spiritual void in my life beyond academics? I began to question *everything*. What was the meaning of life? What was *really* the point? Many nights, I would cry myself to sleep. Too tired to pray, too exhausted to cry out, all I could utter to God was,

"I'm tired."

I spent much of my time after high school graduation pondering my religious experience up until this point. "Jesus loves you." Whenever I heard that phrase in the church, I would cringe and roll my eyes because I felt that it was a waste of time to repeat such obvious truths when we could spend time addressing topics that weren't so obvious. "You are God's child" was another common "cliché" that I would hear all the time. "Duh," I thought, "we are all God's children." I grew up in the church. I got saved at age eight. I have been singing in the choir since before I can remember. My parents became missionaries, and we moved to Cape Town, South Africa when I was ten. When we moved back to the States for my dad to preside over his third church when I was 12, I was even more active. So, whenever I heard the common phrases "You are God's child" or "Jesus loves you," I always thought those to be painfully elementary concepts. Why don't we talk about the bigger stuff, the more important things? But I never really thought about what "love" was or what it meant that Jesus loved me. What did it really mean to be a child of God? What did it truly mean to be a child of the Creator of the Universe?

I always thought that my religion made me right with God. If I cognitively knew the truths of the Bible, then that made me pleasing to God. I believed that the things I did kept me in good standing with Him. If I stayed in church, He loved me. If I didn't show up, He would be disappointed. After all, my earthly father would have a fit if I told him I wasn't going to church anymore. I mean, that makes sense, right? Good works equal entrance into heaven. Every Sunday, I would come to church, and I would pray that He would keep helping me in school, but if I am sincere, there was always a part of me that figured I could do it without Him. I would see people passing out in church, and think, "they are the ones that need Jesus, not me." Yeah, I was struggling with lust that was slowly increasing, but it wasn't affecting me or my relationships. Yeah, I got a little mad, and had fits of rage now and then, but who doesn't fall short of the glory of God, right?

I was wrong. In fact, I have grown to believe that this is one of the most dangerous mindsets to have—that of indifference, passivity, hypocrisy, and lukewarm Christianity. I thought that I was close enough to God to be set for heaven, but I distanced myself just enough so I could keep doing what I wanted. I was always tip-toeing in and out of my faith. I was living a double life. Maintaining a holy appearance and secret sins at the same time. On one hand, I knew I loved God, but as I got older, I began to grow into what felt like contradictions in my identity. Over the course of my gap year after high school graduation, I began to wrestle with my life seriously. Who was I? Who was Nicole? How could I have been so close to God, and yet so far? Over the past years, God has completely changed my view of the gospel to one that I believe more accurately represents Him. Despite the fact I was raised in the church, there was so much more to God that I had yet to experience. Even though I preached, there was so much more freedom that God had for me.

———◆———

When I got into Princeton, the achievement that was supposed to be the culminating success of my first eighteen years of life, left me feeling just as empty as I did before the acceptance letter came. It wasn't until this peak in my academic career that I began to see the vanity of it all. For so long, I had idolized education—it was a major source of self-worth and the reason that I would wake up in the morning. But when I finally got accepted, I got a strong sense that this couldn't be all there was. For this to be supposedly one of my greatest moments, an open door to my future, it didn't feel very exciting. After being accepted to Princeton, I received the opportunity to apply for the school's Bridge Year Senegal program (a nine-month service-learning program sponsored by the University). Though I was initially hesitant to apply because I thought it would take away from my career goals, I ultimately accepted and decided to spend the next academic year of my life in Senegal. Little did I know, that this experience would change my life. Not just because it challenged me intellectually, but it challenged the person that I thought I was. This book is my journey of self-discovery and the revelations I learned along the way.

The love of Jesus has completely transformed my life. My relationship with Him is what enables me to live in a way that is meaningful to me. Now, when I hear the common phrases "Jesus loves you" or "You are God's child," they pierce my heart once again with the love of God. I can't hear them enough. They remind me of my testimony; what God has healed me from and delivered me out of so that I can live an authentic, free, unapologetic life. God wants to fulfill the desires of our hearts. God is loving—He loves us when we are at our worst, even when we are sinning. God does not want to punish us; He does not want to impose excessive regulation on us. He wants us to have fun and enjoy life—this is His heart! I would grow to fall in love with this loving God, not the God of regulations that I thought He was.

Today, it can seem like the church is dying. Breaking news of pastors killing themselves and falling into the same sin they preached against. Subsequently, we see more and more young people leaving the church. Many of us see the church as irrelevant and unnecessary. And yet, the church is the only place where true freedom is offered, because it is where the message of Christ's redemption is preached. I have had the opportunity to attend one of the most prestigious universities in the world, where many people see God as irrelevant, where people have made education their god. In discussions with my peers and professors, I am brought to tears by how misrepresented God and Jesus are by so many proclaimed Christians. But, despite the godlessness I see on my campus, there is still a remnant wholeheartedly seeking God who is daily pursuing a relationship with the God of love, and representing Him to the world. We are the light of the world. We are the salt of the earth.

I believe with all of my heart that God has an excellent purpose and plans for all of us and He wants us to be as free as possible so that we can receive all that He has for us. We all have the capacity to do amazing things in this world—things that our unique personalities, gifts, and experiences enable only us to do. The way that I managed to get out from under the expectations of the world was through building my relationship with God because He is someone who transcends everything here on earth. Why hinder all of our potentials by accepting society's standards and living in fear?

Writing this book is one of the hardest things I have ever done because this is a testimony that has a lot of ugly, and I know in writing this I shatter many people's view of me as "Rev. Williams' daughter," the innocent Nicole who can do no wrong. In my story, you will discover a pastor's daughter who was simultaneously Ivy League-bound and a "woke" Black girl. Someone told by many that she would be successful; someone who prayed for many; someone who preached. And yet, at the same time, you will find someone who attempted suicide at age 12, was bound to a pornography addiction for years and perpetuated anger like it was her middle name. Maybe in writing this, I will now be seen as the PK stereotype, as the preacher's daughter who "lost it" and who is "out there," but I know I also stand as a testament to the redemptive power of the love of God. This book is my testimony; it is my freedom. Alone before God, I had to reconcile the good and the bad, and on His terms, in order to begin living a life that I could truly take pride in. In doing so, I've learned my value and potential. This is my unboxing.

Part 1

---•◆•---

Beautiful Walls

(Church) Family

I couldn't tell you much about that day—who preached, the subject of the sermon, or what made that day any different from every other Sunday. My parents, my two sisters, my brother, and I all sat three aisles from the front like we always did. Nothing about the service particularly stood out. We sang the classic Sunday songs, and the order of service followed the traditional A.M.E. (African Methodist Episcopal) style I had grown used to by age eight. But when the altar call came, unlike most Sundays when I would typically stay put and observe others walking towards the altar, I responded. "If you have yet to give your life to Christ, come to the altar! He wants to use you. He wants to help you." Suddenly, tears began to roll down my eyes. "I need to do this. God wants to use me. I need to have a relationship with Jesus. I need to take the next step." Thoughts began to flood my head that I never had before. Before I knew it, my feet started to move me out of the aisle, and towards the altar. I had already been in the church choir before I could remember. I had recently begun ushering since I became old enough. I always attended Sunday school. I loved singing in church, whether I was in the choir stand or not. The church was home. Bewildered and yet so sure—I walked out of the church that Sunday with my new dedication to Jesus. During the offering, my dad and I were holding hands, dancing together in the pew. I was incredibly joyful that day. As we drove home, I distinctly remember feeling a distinct pride for being a member of the Williams Family. We were Christians, we went to church, and I loved my church community.

All of my life, I grew up in a very loving household. My parents always supported my dreams and aspirations. From changing sports in elementary school to choosing a college, my parents have always been there. They have been my role models of what it means to be Christian, to be a Black American, and more importantly, what it means to be a good human being. My mom has modeled what it means to express unconditional love, to be a woman of God, to serve your community, and to look good while doing it. My dad has shown me how to persevere through hard circumstances, what a man of God looks like, and how to live in a world that will not always love you.

I am the oldest of four siblings. My sister Sarah who is now 16, my sister Hannah, age 13, and my little brother Sidney, age 11, who we nicknamed Wil. We all grew up in a three-story home on the Potomac River in Fort Washington, Maryland until I was ten years old. We lived in one of the most affluent Black middle-class areas in the country. My parents sent me to the best preschool in the country, and one of the best elementary schools. Whenever we got home from school or Sunday's church service, we had the option of playing in the backyard with the playground set, going to one of our two playrooms, or going to one of the two living rooms to watch TV. My siblings and I had everything we could possibly imagine. If there was something we wanted, my dad would almost always say yes. My parents, coming from households where they were deprived of so many childhood joys, did everything in their power to ensure we had everything we wanted. Of course, this lifestyle costs money, and so my parents worked endlessly to maintain it for us. To make up for their absence, they hired a full-time nanny and housekeeper. My siblings and I wanted for nothing and had almost zero responsibility when it came to chores or anything else. Our life was easy. At such a young age, I was not aware of what my parents endured in order to maintain this "easy" life for us. This was all I knew; it was the standard way of living that I assumed everyone experienced.

———————◆———————

As the oldest, I had to be the example for the rest of my siblings and take partial responsibility for their behavior, especially in public. I believe having these responsibilities from a young age is part of the reason for my Type-A personality today. My dad loves to tell the story of the time when I complained to my teachers about having to change my siblings' diapers, even though we had a nanny at the time. Even when I didn't have any real work, I always felt a responsibility for my siblings. I would consistently do my best to make sure they were in line. If daddy left us with chores, I would monitor my siblings and ensure they were doing their part. Even when my parents did not ask, I would reinforce the rules they set. "Wil! You can't play Xbox until you have finished your homework," I would declare to my brother.

"I finished it already." He would half reply as he focused on his Madden NFL Football game.

"Let me check it," I would respond, knowing that he probably did not finish all of his homework. I would often "harass" my brother (as my mom likes to refer to it) during the academic year, as well as much of the summer. During the summer, I would give him extra work so that he could be ahead of his grade. In hindsight, I do wish that I was more relaxed with him; Black men get enough societal pressure as it is but I always wanted the best for him. The Williams Family name meant something, and we all had to play our part to uphold it.

My mom always says I set the bar incredibly high– maybe too high; she'd often add in jokingly. My sister Sarah and I are two years apart, so she feels the pressure to live up to my example the most.

3

I took four Advanced Placement classes my junior year, so she felt she had to take 5. I didn't do sports, so she had to do two sports. I got into an Ivy, and now the expectation is that she must also do the same. None of this is explicitly stated, but it is an unspoken rule in our house that you push yourself as much as you can to reach your full potential. We all strive to do our very best, and we have, for the most part, been the better for it.

No matter how busy all of our lives get, however, the Williams Family always goes to church every Sunday. All of us, together. This has been an important aspect of our family culture that I used to count the number of church days I missed. Before junior year, I could count 5 absences since the age of eight. I had only missed 5 days of the church in my entire life—at least the ones that I had remembered to count. I prided myself on this fact. Even when I went away during the summers, without my parents, I still made my way to church. Little did I know, a relationship with God is so much deeper than church and so much more constant than Sundays.

Black Kid, White World

Our parents intentionally raised us in Fort Washington so that we would have exposure to the vast complexity and prosperity of Black life. At a young age, they aimed to expose us to other prosperous Black families. They wanted us to feel as if our Blackness would not be a limitation to what we could do in life. Of course, Blackness brought its own set of challenges, but it was not synonymous with poor, uneducated, or unsuccessful. We could be all that we wanted to be in life. While I, without a doubt, subconsciously received the message that I could be anything I wanted, their efforts in making me conscious of my Blackness and its normality seemed to escape me. Their efforts couldn't overcome the subtle messages I was receiving from my environment and the broader culture of society at large. I would struggle with my racial identity for the majority of my childhood and teen years.

Because my parents worked so hard to create a different, better life for my siblings and me than what they were raised with as kids, we were very isolated from our extended family. Most of my father's family lived across the South and my mom's family, while they also lived in Maryland, lived at least an hour away. The extended family that I saw most frequently was on my mother's side since they also lived in Maryland, but we did not visit them often. My grandma lived about 45 minutes away so we would visit her several times throughout the year. I don't have much memory of these visits, but I do have very distinct memories of her annual Christmas Eve party.

Every year my grandma would hold an annual Christmas Eve party at her house, and all of my mother's aunts and uncles and their families would do their best to attend. Most of the people at this party, with the exception of me, my siblings, my parents, and my grandma's current husband (my step-grandfather), were white. I have a distinct memory of feeling incredibly out of place. Everyone seemed so different and for years I struggled to understand how we could be related. Not only did we have different skin colors, but our lives also seemed to be very different. My second cousins were volleyball stars, my great aunt and uncle were the outdoorsy type who always went on crazy road trips, and my other great uncle went to Harvard. I never felt comfortable and I never felt myself. A large part of this was because I was only around nine years old when I became conscious of the difference, but during these parties, I always became aware and conflicted about my race. Somehow during my childhood, I developed the subconscious belief that Black was a bad thing to be. This subconscious belief, combined with the experiences I would have on Christmas Eve caused me to eventually develop the impression that I was also white. Because many of my friends from private school and my grandmother were white, I wanted to believe that I was too. At the same time, I was also very conscious of my Blackness at the party. I thought I was white because my grandma was white and yet, in my thirteen-year-old mind, I knew I didn't belong because I was Black. Christmas Eve with my extended family at my grandma's house was probably one of the most confusing events for my racial identity as a child. While we lived in a majority Black, upper-class neighborhood, I only remember a white neighbor, Asian neighbors, and two Black families. Having no real bearings on what race was or its implications, I could not understand how, despite having all of these white family members, I was still Black. My mother, the product of my white grandmother and Black grandfather (my grandmother's ex-husband), was the only thing that linked us together. Everyone was white with the exception of my parents, my siblings, and my grandma's husband. At the same time, I felt like the culture, ways of life, and ways of speaking were all very different from mine.

My maternal grandfather lived about twenty minutes away from my grandma, as well as many of my aunts and cousins. This was my mom's Black side. Everyone was Black with the exception of my grandad's second wife. This environment was extremely different. There was a formality lacking in these family gatherings in comparison to the dinner party at my grandma's. At my grandad's house, I very much felt the cultural difference. Many of my family members on my grandad's side also talked differently. Most of them were not college-educated and spoke with a lot more slang. There was more music and many of the adults outside having "adult conversation," as my mom liked to characterize it every time I would try to sit with her. I was always encouraged to spend time with my cousins, but I never felt close to them. We only saw them around the holidays and it seemed as if we had nothing in common. I remember sitting in the living room, desperately wanting to go home. Eventually, towards the end of our time at our grandad's, Sarah and I would get comfortable enough to have fun, but it took hours to adjust to the environment. Here, I felt out of place for very different reasons. I felt comfortable in my Blackness, but extremely uncomfortable in what I felt was my whiteness. I didn't feel "Black enough" for this family, and I didn't want to be. In hindsight, I subconsciously thought that I was better than them, and wanted very little association with them. Up until the end of middle school, I would battle with the reconciliation of these two worlds, never really understanding what race even was. Every year during the holiday season, when we visited these two very different worlds, I would feel out of place in both.

Perfect Preacher's Kid

My racial identity may have been confusing to understand, but church definitely was not. The familiarity of our church routine all changed when my father answered the call to ministry in 2009. One day when I got home my parents sat us down for some big announcement. I knew my parents were talking about doing missions and my father potentially changing his career goals, but I never expected what would come to pass, and the implications it would have on my future.

"Kids, we are moving to Cape Town, South Africa to do missions work," my dad announced in excitement.

"Your dad has been called to ministry" my mom chimed in.

At nine years old, my family and I moved to Cape Town, South Africa to do mission work. My father was now an investment banker turned pastor, and my siblings and I were now the preacher's kids (PKs). We would move from the third pew to the first. When my parents first told my siblings and me the news, I didn't realize that "PK" encompassed many specific expectations, but as I got older, I would soon learn that it did. Even before my dad's change in career, people would often comment on how beautiful our family was. From a young age, I was very aware that people looked up to my parents and our family as an example. I never thought much of it; if anything, I enjoyed it. Women at church were always coming up to me, smiling, hugging, and asking about school. I felt the overwhelming love in church environments, but with this love and admiration—especially now as a PK, came an inexplicit pressure to perform.

When I was eleven years old (2011), my father accepted a church in Morristown, New Jersey. Morristown would be the last place my family would move until the writing of this book. Here, in a predominantly white town, I would grow to better understand race and my racial identity. It was here that I would grow to become much of the person I am today. I developed many of my passions. I would join various choirs and develop my passion for singing —both within my church and in the community. Morristown would be the home of my middle and high school education. I would co-found a Christian group in my high school and become a leader for racial justice. It is also the place where my identity as a PK would solidify itself.

While my parents never explicitly pressured me to meet any standards as a PK, I put pressure on myself to behave a certain way to ensure that my family was well represented. I often heard stories of other PK's who had gone "off the rails" and I was determined not to be one of them. I did not want to be the stereotypical emotionally suppressed PK. I knew that people were watching our family and I didn't want to be the reason for people talking negatively about us. When my dad ran for political office, a woman from our church lied about my dad having a second family in Cape Town. It was bad enough that people made things up, I didn't want to give any real proof of dysfunction. I wanted my dad to be proud of me, and the community to be proud of him. I strove for perfection. As a PK, I learned to always respect the elders, always smile, and be friendly with everyone. Don't share family business, not even with your friends in church. Don't party, don't drink, don't hang out with the wrong crowd. Definitely, don't have sex or date. Do well in school. As I was used to doing from a young age, I actively participated in the church through choir, dance, teaching Sunday school, the multimedia ministry, and even as a preacher. I preached every couple of years beginning at age twelve. At fifteen years old, I was licensed as an exhorter in the AME Church. I was even afforded the opportunity to preach at a church in Boston when I was there for a summer at the age of 15.

Between 2014 and 2016, I preached several sermons all surrounding the topic of worthiness and self-love in the eyes of God. I felt passionate about this issue and wanted to share about it through sermons entitled "Beautiful Me," "Naturally Me," and "You're Worthy." In the sermon, I entitled "You're Worthy, Word for Word," I said, "Even though we know God loves us and we know He will always be there for us, we just don't feel valued; but we must remember that worldly things are temporary and God's love is eternal. We don't have to be another suicidal statistic, we are more worthy, we are more worthy than 1,000 sparrows, and God inhabits the praises of his people." I was preaching God's truth but I was blind to how much I wasn't fully living in these truths. Even with the knowledge and courage to preach, I still allowed myself to be distracted by my insecurities. I would teach about how the essence of our being is in God, and that is our first and foremost identity. I look back on these accomplishments and have great joy but I also grieve at how much pain I was in without even realizing it. On the outside, it seemed like all was well, but my life on the inside was an entirely different story.

Part 2

On the Inside

Insecure

While I took my role as a PK very seriously, as I reflect on the two-year transition from moving to South Africa and ultimately moving back to the United States, it took a deep toll on my emotional and mental health and my sense of belonging. The move to South Africa meant leaving everything I knew: my friends, my room, my clothes, my grandparents, my favorite foods, and entering a foreign land for "missions." It all happened so fast, that I don't know if I even had time to fully understand what was happening, but the next thing I knew, I was in a new school, a new home, a new church, and a new environment with new people.

Before moving to South Africa, I had my two best friends and we would hang out all the time. I still remember running around during elementary school recess, exchanging secrets, and giggling at each other's jokes. From what I can remember, I felt love. I felt acceptance. I felt at peace. I would go home knowing that I had a world at school full of joy, even if the home didn't always feel that way. Within a matter of months, my entire world changed. On my first day at the new school, I was a ball of anxiety. I was so afraid that people wouldn't like me, and I wasn't sure if I would even like them. Despite my hesitation, months passed and I learned to love my peers and teachers. I grew close with my class. Recess there became just as comfortable, free, and loving as recess back in my old hometown.

One day at recess, John (one of the boys in my class) calls my close friend Lisa to talk to her. Apparently, he had a "message" for me from Joshua. As elementary crushes go, Joshua revealed to me through a series of trusted friends that he had liked me since the first day I got to the school. I had never experienced this before. Butterflies filled my stomach. That Friday I went home bubbly, happy, and in anticipation of the next week with this newfound information. Unaware of how "love" or "liking" worked, I was excited for my *future* with Joshua.

When I went home, my parents had another announcement for my siblings and me. "Kids, we are putting you in a new school…." As my father continued speaking, my world sank. I had finally made friends! I had finally become comfortable. I had moved past all my anxiety and fear and created a *family* at my school. On top of that, I had a future with Joshua to plan! Luckily, I was able to have a goodbye play date with Lisa but I didn't get a chance to formally say goodbye to Joshua or the rest of my friends before I left my new home to face another new world.

This new school was worse for me socially than the last—bigger, with more prestige, more money, and a sea of international students in navy blue uniforms—I was deadly afraid. If I was a ball of anxiety before, words could not express the dread I felt now. Once a lover of soccer and recess activities, I sat on the sidelines. I felt like everyone was talking about me, everyone was judging me, and everyone hated me. I just wanted to go back to any of my previous schools! I desperately longed for belonging. To make matters worse, my fourth-grade teacher skipped me to fifth grade. If I thought people were staring and talking about me before, I was sure that they definitely were now. Sitting in *another* new classroom full of fifth-graders just weeks into my new school, I wanted to disappear. I wished I had never existed.

Along with the move to a new school, we moved houses at the same time. Whereas our first house was furnished, our new house had no furniture with the exception of two beds and a plastic table and chairs. This house would remain unfurnished until our return back to the States. When I left school, I went to a house that did not feel like home in the slightest. Nowhere was safe. The world around me was the only world I now knew and not only was it foreign but it was cold, isolating, and unwelcoming in every way possible. As a child, I changed schools four times within the span of a year and a half. Each time I moved, feelings of loneliness and anxiety would increase.

When we finally moved back to the United States when I was eleven, like most girls in their preteen years, I began to become body-conscious. Flooded with images in the media of skinny, white, beautiful, long-haired girls, I slowly but surely began to despise my own body. I felt fat, and I felt ugly. Already feeling like an outsider and beginning to feel the additional societal pressures to meet a certain standard of beauty, I became extremely insecure in not only who I was, but also how I looked. Now suddenly back in the States, I felt utterly confused. Our new home was located in Morristown, New Jersey. It was my home country, but it was not the Fort Washington, Maryland I had lived my first nine years of life. I was happy, mostly because my parents were happy, but the undercurrent of isolation, anxiety and insecurity that had grown during my time in Cape Town continued to consume me and take up more and more of my thought life. I felt like I had to change myself in order to belong. Moving to so many schools, crossing so many cultures, and balancing that with discovering my own identity was extremely difficult.

On top of that, I was the kid fresh off the boat from Africa. "Do you speak African? Did you see lions? Did you live in huts?" were just a few of the questions I would receive on a daily basis in my first few months in Morristown. I maintained the same defense mechanisms as I did in my second school in Cape Town. I didn't talk. I only spoke when spoken to. I hated where I had come from and I hated who I was because I despised the feeling of being different.

Everything about me—past and present, everything I did seemed to be wrong. I was insecure about *everything* about myself. As I aimed to make sense of my life up to this point and my future, my experiences made me feel as if I was replaceable, and the world would go on better without me. All of this was an inner turmoil I never voiced to anyone, not even with my family or friends. It wasn't that I didn't trust them, but I felt like I had to deal with it on my own in order to prove I was strong. I thought that admitting my weakness would somehow only make matters worse. It was my issue to handle.

My experiences at home and at school made me feel unlovable and unworthy of living. I began to believe that God did not have a purpose for my life. The girl who had given her life to God at age eight, no longer felt like God was in her life—or if He was, He simply didn't care enough. Life began to seem so dismal, that I created a narrative in my head that if I committed suicide before I turned thirteen, I would go to heaven. Suicidal thoughts continued to build up until I couldn't fight them anymore. Not only did I not think my life was important, but I also didn't feel worthy of life. On one fateful evening, I tried to leave all of the painful realities of my world. At just 12 years old, I attempted to take my life.

While everyone was out of the house, I decided, "I am going to kill myself!" As I paced my room, fed up with everything, hopeless thoughts flooded my head. I can't do it anymore. I hate my life. Nobody cares about me. I'll make them wish they cared. I'll never be anything in life anyway. I thought about all the ways I could do it: a knife, pills, water.... Water! Electricity... the radio! I had contemplated suicide before but this time I was serious. Frantically, I ran to the bathroom and began running the bath water. I searched my room for my radio. I plugged the radio into the bathroom wall but realized the cord was not long enough to reach the bathtub. No! What can I do? How will I escape? I returned to my room. What was I to do now? I guess I'll have to keep living. I had this irrational fear that my parents would find out what I had tried to do. Fearing what my dad would do the most, that night I prayed...

Dear God,

I pray that you keep my dad from ever finding out about my suicide attempt. I promise I won't try it again. Amen.

I didn't want my dad to find out because I was afraid he would punish me for it. Despite being a daddy's girl, my dad and I did not have the best relationship growing up. I carried inexplicable resentment against my dad because I often felt like his rage towards me was irrational and undeserved. It seemed he was always angry with me, even when I didn't do anything wrong. I can't even remember what I did to cause the punishment. All I can remember is that afterward, I felt lonely. I felt like a failure. I would often joke to my siblings and my mom, "Daddy hates me." I felt like no matter what I did, my dad wasn't satisfied with my efforts. I always admired the freedom it seemed like my siblings had, and I resented my dad for giving me so many responsibilities as his first child. I felt like who I was, was simply not good enough, that it would never be good enough to please my dad. I thought that if he found out about my suicide, I would be a disappointment to him.

Having made the promise to God not to attempt suicide again, I felt I had to keep it. Lying in bed, feeling trapped in my body, and what made up my 12 years of life, I desperately hoped for a way out. Since suicide was no longer an option, I wondered what would lie ahead. Days turned into weeks and weeks into months and months into years, and the suicide attempt disappeared, under the rug—no one ever found out. It was all a blur... something to be forgotten. God had answered my prayer: my dad never found out about my suicide attempt. So as I promised God, I never tried to commit suicide again, but I still had to figure out how to live. You would hope that I would seek God for answers, but to my own demise, I still tried to figure things out for myself.

My feelings of insecurity led me to feel trapped and afraid. Still fearing that my parents would discover my suicide attempt, I did my best to make it seem like I was okay. Being at such a low point in my life—alone, depressed, and insecure—I learned to live with and suppress my fears. The feelings of insecurity, anxiety, and being unloved just grew. I didn't die on the night I attempted to take my life, but I did lose my life to something else: fear. Fear took over my life. It became the driving force of many of my decisions. Over the years, I developed methods to deal with my pain, emptiness, and fear, as well as ways to hide it all from others.

Secret Sin

Coming into my preteen years, I became increasingly curious about my sexuality. What exactly was sex? I heard references on TV and jokes in school, but I wasn't even sure what it was. I knew it wasn't something to ask my parents. In church, sex seemed like an untouchable subject. If you weren't married, you shouldn't even be thinking about it—let alone *talking* about it. Who could I ask? Who could I ask and not be ashamed to ask? I felt like I would be judged if I asked anyone I knew. My parents were out of the question, people at church—definitely no, and I didn't have any friends I felt comfortable asking. What if they would think I was stupid for not knowing? Finally, the answer came, I would ask Google. Surely, Google would have all the answers.

"Sex" is what I would type into Google. I slowly began to understand what sex was. A man and a woman.... Oh.... Wow... As I continued my search I began to see the word "porn". What was porn? Suddenly, I was on a "porn" website with thousands of videos of people having sex. What was this? One by one, I began to watch the videos. The people seemed to really be enjoying themselves. From all that time in church, I knew watching this was probably a sin of some sort, but it seemed okay in the moment. I closed the tabs with my newfound knowledge of sex and pornography. Little did I know, my one-word Google search would turn into something much greater.

Weeks passed after the day of my research, and the thought to watch the videos again entered my head. I googled the pornographic website name I had remembered from the last time. At the same time that I was striving to be the perfect "Preacher's Kid," I was slowly developing a pornography addiction.

When I entered high school I had to manage the stress of an unrealistic course load. Pornography entered my life to give me temporary relief. My need for escape was at an all-time high. Since getting off this "hamster wheel of life" wasn't an option, my addiction to pornography dramatically increased. When I was using pornography, in those moments, I could forget everything else about my life. In the same way, I used social media and Netflix, I could think about other people, rather than thinking about my own situation. In a way, pornography was a form of security. I knew that it would always be there.

"I hate myself. I am disgusting. There's no hope for me." This was my predominant belief for about two years. No one would ever love me or care if they knew what I was doing behind closed doors. My low self-esteem only worsened as the addiction became more pervasive in my life. "Nicole never does anything wrong, she's just a child." These were the opinions my friends would often voice around me. "What does she know about sex?" I felt like my life carried so much secrecy. With people, I had one persona. Alone, I was a different person— someone with hundreds of sexual images replaying in my mind. I also felt even worse about my body. Seeing all of these women with perfect thin, hourglass figures, made me feel even uglier. *Why couldn't I be like them?* I felt trapped. I wanted to escape but I didn't know how; I was so disgusted with myself, and I didn't even think any relief was possible.

To meet the demands of my addiction, I was always trying to isolate myself. "I'm busy, leave me alone" was a phrase I used all too often at home. The addiction began to push me away from family and friends. I passed up opportunities to spend time with people so I could watch porn instead.

My method for escaping the realities of life only perpetuated my emptiness. Feeling like my outside persona was a lie and isolating myself from friends, my social anxiety also began to increase. I would always feel like someone knew, or that one day I would get caught and have to explain what I was doing. I was constantly thinking of ways to seem like I wasn't doing what I was doing, but couldn't think of any persuasive excuses. I did my best to maintain my secrecy but I was living in perpetual anxiety about someone finding out about the "real me." The anxiety only drove me further into the addiction as I used porn as a means to escape anxiety. It was a never-ending cycle. One of the scariest parts of it all, looking back on it now, is how much denial I used to justify my habit. All of the media I consumed told me it was okay, and so I continued despite all of its obvious negative effects.

When I finally did come to acknowledge how much it was hurting me, I felt powerless in overcoming it. My desire for pornography gradually increased. Once a week had become a couple of times a week. Months had turned into years and a couple of times a week turned into a couple of times a day. Now that I wanted to stop, it seemed impossible. What was initially a place to relieve stress and escape the realities of life slowly evolved into an all-consuming addiction. I found myself not actually desiring to watch porn but going to it simply out of habit. I couldn't stop. I would pray to God afterward and tell him how sorry I was. For years I felt shame about my sexuality. I felt ashamed for having sexual desires. The shame I carried just pushed me deeper into the cycle. I promised I would never do it again, and then a couple of days later I fell subject to the same sin. I slowly stopped praying because I felt like there was no point. I knew that I would just fail to meet my promises and disappoint God, again. Though I never consciously voiced it, I grew to feel that He simply wanted nothing to do with me, the same sentiment I held when I attempted to take my life all those years ago.

Double Identity

Those Christmas Eve dinners at grandma's house influenced me a lot more than I realized. When high school came, and I found myself searching for an identity, things got complicated. Growing up, I always thought of myself as white because to be Black was to be uneducated and ugly. I never consciously thought this, but the belief was there, still replaying itself in the subconscious of my mind. At the beginning of high school, I began to be more conscious of my racialized self-hate. Striving to understand who I really was, I consumed myself with what I would learn to be the beauty of black culture. I ran to my Blackness, desperately wanting it to be my savior from whiteness, from my double consciousness, and from my self-hatred.

In my freshman year of high school, YouTube exposed me to the natural hair world. In a video, a woman explained that she decided to do the "big chop" in 2009 and "go natural" because she was tired of her relaxer. Having gotten relaxers for a year or so and always having my hair straightened, I didn't think that there was another way of doing hair. In this video, the Youtuber stood in her bathroom with an India Arie song playing in the background and proceeded to cut off her relaxed hair. This clip was followed by a progression of pictures over the course of five years after her big chop. She now had long, curly, beautiful hair. I was astonished. I wanted this! I wanted to have my natural hair. My straightened hair had always been something I had liked, but I wanted something different. The woman in the video also talked about wanting to be her natural self, and that included the way she wore her hair. I figured that if I went natural, then I could "find myself" too. Inspired by the natural hair movement, and in a desperate attempt to love myself authentically, I decided to go natural. Without consulting my parents, I borrowed hair scissors from a friend, went to my bathroom, and began cutting away the relaxed hair. In the end, I was left with a small Afro.

When my dad found out I cut all of my "beautiful" hair off, he was extremely concerned—he deemed me either depressed or insane. Too afraid to admit the real root of why I cut my hair—that I didn't love myself and desperately wanted to, I insisted that I liked my hair this way. I claimed that I was trying to embrace the real me, but he didn't agree with how I went about it. In addition to my dad's reservations, not many people liked my new style. I'd once had "good hair" and suddenly chose to get rid of it. In hindsight, my Afro wasn't that cute, and I had no idea how to style it, but I was so desperate to find identity and significance and worth, that I didn't care. Over the years, I would learn to style my hair, but within those first few months, despite my best efforts, my insecurity worsened. It was my most effort to escape, and I had failed. I still styled my natural hair but I never really loved it. Whenever I had a significant event, I would straighten my hair. My natural hair never felt authentically mine. I was stuck between this tension of trying to embrace my Blackness and simultaneously trying to love myself. I wanted to love myself through the lens of my Black identity as if that was the only relevant identity in my life, and it left me feeling the same emptiness that I had felt before I cut my hair. It was a scary thing to be a young person just trying to find themselves and getting entangled in the complexities of race.

In my desperate attempts to embrace my Blackness, I failed to face many realities: for one, conditioning doesn't just go away, and culture isn't an outfit you can put on. I would embrace my Blackness but only on the surface. There was still a deep-seated part of me that thanked God for light skin, light eyes, and a looser curl pattern. There was always that part of me that felt grateful to have a white grandmother. I hated that I thought these things, but rather than confronting them, I just buried them inside and worked to hide them in the way that I conducted myself. I felt like I had to apologize for my whiteness. I threw myself into the fight for social justice as a way to relieve myself from the guilt of my whiteness. I tried to immerse myself in "Black culture" by listening to trap music and trying to change the way I spoke. Aware of what I perceived as two conflicting cultures within me, I became a walking manifestation of double consciousness. When I was with my white friends, I automatically switched into a white persona—a softer voice, passive opinions, intensely kind and submissive to whatever they wanted. If they wanted me to "act Black", I would do so. If I knew my Blackness made them uncomfortable, I would toe it down. When I was with my Black friends—well I didn't have any. My best friend was Black, but she shared the burden of being raised in a white world, constantly pressured to reject our Blackness. All I knew was whiteness and by extension that influenced my culture. I knew very little about what "Black culture" was, in all its facets and complexity.

I lived in this box of continually trying to fit somewhere when it came to my racial identity. I wanted to fit in a white world, but I never felt accepted because of my appearance. I tried to fit in a Black world, but I felt like I didn't know the culture and that I couldn't relate to "real" Black people.

———— • ————

Sophomore year of high school I began to educate myself on racial injustice in the United States. With this, I became more aware of how white-washed I was in my thinking and in the subconscious views I held about my Blackness. I became conscious of my negative self-image and internalized anti-Blackness imposed on me by the media. My world history teacher had us read the definitions of white and Black in the dictionary. White had strong associations with goodness and purity. Black had all of the associations of evil and danger. I had never realized how negative my images were of Blackness and how positive my images were of whiteness. Now aware of this, I worked to deconstruct my views of beauty and learn new ways of thinking. I read about other Black women who learned to love their Blackness from their mind to their skin to their natural hair and tried to follow in their footsteps. More conscious about the political implications of the natural hair movement, I grew to love my Afro and invested in all the natural products. I saw it as a symbol of resisting systemic oppression and embracing Blackness. I still would straighten my hair for important events, but I loved what my natural hair symbolized. I would walk down the halls of my high school with a new boldness. I was Black and Black was beautiful. I still struggled with body image but I no longer, at least consciously, felt ashamed of my Blackness.

Coming into my increased racial awareness, I began to find a strong sense of identity and purpose within my Blackness. In class, my peers knew me as the girl who always "made everything about racism" and "just couldn't get over it." Since I had a new understanding of the history of my ancestors that school never taught me, I would present this information in class whenever I felt like my history was being under or misrepresented. I had a purpose, a significant role to play. I liked it.

When some seniors in my high school started a group for African Americans, I joined my junior year—excited to be in a community with my people. With this newfound identity, I also felt a call to join the fight. What started as a safe space for African American students, a friend and I turned into a social activism club: Melanin Minds. Our club was hugely successful. We got our high school to create a more inclusive history curriculum, organized a Political Awareness Day and had weekly meetings to educate students about the realities of racial inequality that plagued our community and our high school. We started a conversation about tough, triggering topics—we woke people up.

So consumed in all of my efforts, though, I began to take even less care of myself. I would spend hours preparing presentations, doing research, creating lessons, networking outside of our high school, and so much more. I was fighting the good fight against racial injustice at the expense of my health. In addition to school demands, I now had to meet the demand of creating racial justice within my high school. During Melanin Mind's busiest times of the year, I would be lucky if I got two to three hours of sleep every night. I ate to manage the stress, and so my eating habits worsened. Within a couple of months, I had gained twenty more pounds. My fight was weighing me down.

———◆———

My dissatisfaction with the realities of injustice, while it first drove me to work hard, ultimately manifested itself as anger. While the efforts with Melanin Minds were tremendous and we created radical change within my high school that would inspire more change after I left, I developed righteous anger against everyone who I perceived as a hindrance to our goal of racial equality. However, this anger began to consume me and began to morph into bitterness. Because I was already hurting from other things in my life, much of the suppressed dissatisfaction I was already feeling from the relationship with my dad would play into my anger when it came to racial injustice. I would walk into school feeling like I was in a war. I perceived white people as inherently problematic. Having to deal with the implicitly racist things white people would say stressed me out. I would rant in frustration to my friends about how blind white people were. I carried a bitter resentment against them for their ignorance. Day to day, I would harbor so much resentment against the pervasive ignorance and lack of awareness in my high school. Even more so, being the spokesperson for the realities of Black life in my classrooms gave me a sense of superiority around anyone who was ignorant of race issues. Everything was white or Black; either you were for racial equality or against it. If you were for it, I expected you to speak out. If you were against it, I was determined to make you see the flaws in your ways. Every time I entered a conversation about race, it was a battle that I was determined to win. The very reality of the threats to Blackness in society was by extension very real threats to my very existence since I perceived my identity to be fully defined by my Blackness. Therefore, I developed indignation and hatred toward white systems of oppression, white people, and anyone who threatened my fight for racial equality. I was incapable of loving anyone with a different view than mine and I had a very cynical view of the world.

Not only was I fighting people on a daily basis, but I was also fighting those who had great potential to help the cause. Because my Blackness was my sole source of identity, I thought anything threatening Blackness was a threat to my existence that must be dealt with. As a result, I perceived white people as the "problem." Rachel, who was a white-passing, biracial peer of mine was s who could have been a great friend, and an even greater ally to our movement for social justice, but I turned her into an enemy.

We ran into each other at a cafe in town. Rachel went to a different high school but she overheard me talking about race in America with a friend, and she wanted to participate in the conversation. She seemed friendly; I could tell she was Black but also white-passing. I immediately assumed that she identified as Black. We discussed how racism was a political construct and I casually mentioned that you are either Black or white, you can't be both, assuming that Rachel would agree with me. She stopped me.

"Wait, what? I am not Black or white; I am biracial. I am Black and white." I rolled my eyes.

"Rachel, you can't be both; that is not how the system works. You have to choose," I blatantly responded without even thinking twice.

"No," she snapped back. We went back and forth about our beliefs until finally, she broke down in tears. At that point, I didn't even care. I was infuriated. I couldn't understand how she should be so ignorant. Even after that conversation in which we were on very opposing sides of an argument, Rachel and I would go back and forth between trying to be friends and hating each other.

Today it saddens me that I fought her so much. I was not able to have any compassion for her. Even if I was right, how could I have been so cruel? I brought her to tears. I didn't realize it then, but to her, it felt as if I was attacking her very existence. It was as if I was saying as a person she did not exist because she didn't fit into a box, the same way society made me feel I didn't exist because I *did* fit into the "Black box."

Feeling insecure in my own identity, I felt her existence was a direct threat to mine. Her racial identity as "biracial" threatened the boundaries of the racial construct that I spent much of my life working within. I felt like she had to be "Black" or "white" and there was no in-between. In essence, I could not tolerate the "grayness" of her identity. In my racial worldview, you were either Black, or you were white. While I do believe that race is a political construct and

what matters is what you look like, I used what the racial construct
said and made that the Universal Truth of how one racially identifies,
rather than acknowledging the complexities of racial identity and
acknowledging the realities of Rachel's life existing in the middle of
these two identities. I was extremely mean to Rachel and I showed
no respect for her or her opinions. I perpetuated the same hurt that
I was trying to protect myself from. I was mean to Rachel because
I hated the gray in my own identity. Here I was, fighting for racial
justice, trying to make up for the fact that I came from privilege and
my grandmother was white. I hated my whiteness in an effort to
reclaim my Blackness. I couldn't stand someone who decided to live
in both identities simultaneously. I wasn't just mad at Rachel because
her biracial identity "threatened the cause," I was mad because her
identity threatened who I was because I didn't know who I was. I never
felt oppressed growing up. I never grew up feeling like a member of a
marginalized group because of my race until middle school, and even
then my fight was internal—no one ever told me I needed to look a
certain way, and no one ever bullied me. The racism I experienced was
internalized; I was fighting myself. Melanin Minds gave me a platform
to channel my own self-hate into righteous anger against the system.
This all gave way to an isolating lifestyle in which my rage would slowly
kill me. I thus literally became an "angry Black woman," incapable of
loving those with different views than mine. I didn't know how to love;
I had not yet even learned what it meant to love myself.

In "Love"

"I love you." We sat at a restaurant and he looked deep into my eyes.
This scared me. I honestly believed that no one could ever love me—I
wasn't pretty enough, I was obese, I talked too much, I was annoying.
Why would anyone fall in love with me? Nonetheless, Sam was a guy
that I also had a lot of admiration for. We had been friends for a long
time, and if I was being completely honest, I also began to see him
as more than a friend. Love scared me and when he told me, I had

no idea what to do. I liked him, but I didn't even know how to love myself. How could I possibly love him? I wasn't really sure what it meant to love. I knew it was impossible for me to be in a relationship with him because I would become dependent on him for validation. We ultimately decided to stay friends, as hard as that decision was.

I wish I could tell you that was all that happened, but in the days following his proclamation of love, we would be more than just friends. One night, I got close to losing my virginity. I am glad to say that I kept my virginity during a period in my life when I was playing with fire, but I began to give up parts of myself in return for the momentary feeling of being loved. Although it may seem like it, my intention in writing this is not to spite my pastor-father. I want to be completely honest because I know I am not the only one to go through something like this. For one, my sexual curiosity was suppressed at a young age and its inevitable manifestation became my introduction to pornography. As the pastor's daughter, I was perceived as "pure," and unable to commit the "most vile" sin. In the same way, the things I did gave me significance, the things I didn't do made me feel equally good about myself. I felt that when it came to my sexuality, as long as I didn't date or have sex, I was pure. Meanwhile, my mind could run rampant with sexual impurity and I could maintain my pornography addiction. As long as I didn't "do it," I was in the clear.

Being a human being designed *for* love, I began to seek out love in all the wrong places. I grew up in a household that emphasized the importance of purity. I agreed with the principal, but in practice, I was already someone with a pornography addiction. I already felt like my purity was long gone. My mind had been tainted by so many sexual images. On top of that, I didn't love myself or recognize my own worth. Mainstream culture told me through years of passively watching TV shows and movies that I could find love through relationships, more specifically sexual relationships. As I got older, despite my own insecurity, men began to be interested in me. Because of the pornography addiction, I was largely desensitized to what I believe today to be the sacredness of sex. Even as I began the Holy

Spirit began to teach me the importance of purity, I couldn't shake the subconscious notion ingrained in my mind that sex simply wasn't a big deal. Even as I would grow to understand God's grace, I still felt having sex was the worst thing to do, while simultaneously feeling like it wasn't a big deal. It was this blatant contradiction in my thinking that left me extremely confused when it came to potential romantic relationships. Ironically, the combination of suppression and pressure to meet such high standards of purity pushed me into the pornography addiction and ultimately led to my casual views of sex.

I don't blame *anyone* for the suppression of my sexual curiosity or the expectations of a preacher's daughter. I know that my church family had good intentions in their views of me. I was the one who enabled the label of PK to control the way I acted. I didn't have to accept it, but I chose to because I thought I had to. Many of the expectations of PKs are cultural, and no one person is at fault for perpetuating them. At the same time though, this issue is something the church should work to address. Similarly, sex is, heavily stigmatized in church environments. The Bible says sin is sin. There is no hierarchy, and yet young people, especially girls, are made to feel as if sexual promiscuity is the worst thing in the world. This is the downside of church "purity culture." I am not trying to diminish the significance of sex, but there is so much unnecessary pressure on our young people that affects us far into our adulthood. I was already feeling ashamed about having sexual desires but instead of feeling safe to talk about these things and gain a godly perspective, I turned to society and was led astray.

After that moment, I was utterly confused. *Did I really just do that?* I couldn't have. All of the discussion about the importance of purity in my home and at church, and I had just thrown away so easily. The scariest part was I didn't even feel guilty about it. In fact, I thought about doing it again. I always hated the idea of romantic vulnerability. I thought girls who needed men for love were weak. I used to see girls who hooked up with guys as desperate, and now I was becoming one of them. I desperately wanted to belong and I was looking for any place I could to do so.

Maintenance

As my search for identity and belonging progressed, my roles as a pastor's kid and as a woke Black woman made me feel like I found authentic affirmations of who I was. In each of these identities, there were a series of things I had to do in order to feel significant. As a PK, I had to participate in church, be likable, and simultaneously do well in school. As a woke Black woman, I had to be hyper-conscious about racial issues and fight whenever I saw injustice. All of this striving was driven by a fear of exposure and a need to prove that I was "good" to others.

"What do you want to be when you grow up?" This was the classic question that every young person would get. My parents instilled the value of education in me from a very young age. If we wanted to be successful in life, we would need to go to school and do well. So, as a middle school student, I knew the importance of doing well in school, and always did the best I could. During one of my extracurricular activities, we created vision boards with magazine cutouts. Still unsure of my specific goals, I decided that I would aspire to be "successful" in whatever field I would enter. My parents and other mentors in my life told me that if I wanted to be the best in whatever field I would enter, I should aspire to attend a top undergraduate school. My parents also made it clear that they wouldn't be able to afford my college education; Ivy League schools could potentially give me a full ride. For the next six years, my goal was Harvard—a Mecca of the most successful people.

I worked like there was no tomorrow. In my freshman year, I doubled in French and Latin because I figured Latin would help prepare me for the SAT and French would look good on my transcript. While most students took two electives, my only elective was choir. In my sophomore year, I took two math classes (Geometry and Algebra II) because I had already taken Algebra I as a freshman —all while still doubling in language. During my junior year, I was still taking both AP Latin and AP French, and I also decided to take two histories: AP European History and US History II Honors. My life was a cycle of school, homework, church, and more homework. As a senior, my Advanced Placement courses consisted of AP Calculus A.B., AP Biology, and AP English Literature.

I knew that top schools would want to see that I did something meaningful during my summers. I spent my summers doing extra coursework to get ahead and I even traveled abroad to France. The summer after the end of my sophomore year, I attended the Harvard Summer School Program.

During Harvard's program, I built lifelong friendships, sat in classrooms learning from brilliant minds, and got to live out college life. It was the most amazing experience. The program, as one might expect, was also very intensive. I was taking two courses with papers due almost every week in class. In addition to this course work, I also had summer work for AP English Language, a course I would be taking as a junior. I did my best to manage all of the work, but I ended up putting off most of the AP English work until I got home from Harvard's program. By the grace of God, I managed to finish the assignment and turn it in—it wasn't my best work but I figured it was still quality. A week later, I got the grade back: an 83%. I looked at the grade and cried. I couldn't believe how terribly I had done. While I would later find out that an 83% was actually a "good" grade in her class, I was absolutely devastated. With this being my first grade in the class, I saw it as a sign that I wasn't cut out for this type of work. I figured I wasn't good enough. I considered my Ivy League aspirations long gone. For a week, I was extremely depressed.

As the intensity of high school increased, I would have mental breakdowns either triggered by the stress of school or a "low" grade. One evening every now and then, during a week where I may have gotten a total of 8 hours of sleep, I would look at my long to-do list and just cry and cry and cry. I felt so empty all the time. Anything below an A in a class would be a blow to my self-esteem. I was always anxious about my grades, fearing that one slip-up would ruin all of my dreams. I worked like a slave but I thought it would all be worth it if I got into an Ivy. After every mental breakdown, I would suppress my feelings of emptiness and sadness, and go back to being consumed in the grind. School was my god. I loved the "blessings" of good grades. I abided by its rules. I feared its punishment—the crushing of my academic and career aspirations.

During my junior year, one of my teachers expressed to me that she believed I could make it into an Ivy League school but that my test scores were too low. I was already killing myself, but seeing no other option but to study, my grind radically increased. The first time I took the ACT was June of my junior year: my score? A 26. It was decent, but not nearly what was needed for acceptance into an Ivy League school. Because of my plans for the summer, I barely studied, but I completed the entire Princeton ACT Review book. I figured I would at least bring my score up one point, right?? Nope. To my surprise, my September ACT score was a 24. I wanted to cry; I was absolutely devastated, but after all, I'd been through, I was not going to let this be the reason that prevented me from getting into a top school. Maintaining this workload required radical changes in the way I managed my time. After school I would go home at 2:30, sleep at 4 pm, and wake up between 12 am and 2 pm to do my homework, work on college applications, and study for the ACT. Eventually, I would raise my score to a 29 but it was at an expense. I was always sleep-deprived, I barely spent time with my family, and in the free time I did have I was in my extracurricular activities. I hated the fast pace but in my mind, there was no other option. It was literally make or break. Either I would succeed (get into a top school) or fail (don't get into a top school)—there was no middle ground.

In reality, I used school as a means to escape the emptiness I felt. It enabled me to dream of a better future—one where happiness was never-ending. If I did this, I thought, I could not fail in life. My life would be full of joy and success.

On the track to success, I never dealt with any of the hurt I had experienced—instead, I focused steadfastly on pursuing my goal but the striving only made me feel more empty. I used school as a mask to hide all of the pain I was feeling. I needed it to distract me from feeling my brokenness. Even though I didn't feel it most of the time, people perceived me as smart. Academics was a great source of validation. The better I did in school, it seemed, the more loved I was—especially by myself. If I did well, I could be proud of myself. If I didn't, I would be extremely disappointed in myself. Of course, anytime I was proud of myself, a sense of "You could have done better," would soon follow. The validation was fleeting, so I had to keep working hard to maintain a sense of self-worth. It was a constant cycle that I continuously had to feed.

School also gave me a sense of control. In essence, I could control how good or bad I felt about myself based on how I performed. The feeling of control also gave me a sense of purpose. From day to day, having to organize all of my assignments and coordinate events in my life, I was able to feel powerful, where I might otherwise have felt powerless.

Because academics became a source of self-worth and significance, any holes in my knowledge threatened that security. Thus, I was always working as hard as possible to make sure I knew everything that was being taught to me. If I didn't know something I was already expected to know, I would be driven by deep insecurity to work as hard as possible to learn it. Thus not only was my high school hamster wheel working towards the goal of success, it was also a daily striving for self-worth and a feeling of control. I was trapped in a cycle of needing academics in order to feel good about myself on any given day. Things in my personal life could be going badly, but doing well in school made me feel good about myself, at least in that moment. It was killing me, but it was a means of surviving, and maintaining that facade of the "Perfect Pastor's Kid." My parents could tell something was wrong but I would always tell them I was fine. I didn't have the language to talk about what I was going through and I didn't know how to ask for help.

I needed significance and love, and I thought the only way to get that was through these facades and maintaining arbitrary lines of what it meant to be "good" and "pure." In the midst of following the rules of what it meant to be a "good person," inside I was still that twelve-year-old girl that struggled with body image, feelings of worth, and comparison. On one hand, I never really felt like the beautiful "unapologetic Black woman" that I wanted to be as I led the African American Culture Club. I never really felt like the innocent PK (especially with my secret addiction), and I never really felt smart. On the other hand, I had to put on masks for people to make it seem as if I were all of these things in order to feel good about myself. I felt as if I had to hide the infinite chasm between who I really was and who I was supposed to be. I was Black, and I was white. I listened to trap, I listened to gospel. All of this pressure drove me further into a need to escape through pornography and deeper into isolation. I never told anyone how I really felt, not even my best friend because I thought that even with her, I needed to maintain a certain image. I feared exposure of who I really was when no one was looking: an angry, porn-addicted, insecure teen. Pornography addiction, sexual promiscuity, self-hatred, insecurity, unresolved anger, unforgiveness. Pastor's daughter, Unapologetic Black Woman, role model, community figure, and stellar student. All of these identities and struggles and their intersections confused me; I was a hypocrite.

Many of my passions began to feel like chores; victories felt like opening doors to more work. I no longer felt excited about school or choir—two of the things I once loved. It was during my striving to be the "Perfect Preacher's Kid" that I lived an extremely insecure life. The burden of inadequacy weighed on me and began to reflect in every area of my life. Where I once loved liturgical dance, I grew to despise it because I felt like the dance uniforms made me look fat. I desperately wanted to sing solos in church and yet now perceived choir rehearsals as a chore. Even though I held high leadership positions in the youth ministry, I decided to quit everything. I didn't care about serving God anymore. I just viewed it as something that wasted my time, drained my energy, and made me feel worse about myself. After the failed suicide attempt, I never really dealt with my feelings of insecurity and lack of significance. Of course, I hid it all, like I hid every other struggle. I worked extremely hard to maintain a facade of someone who was secure in who she was, and I only got better at mastering this mask. I continued to come to church and work hard in school. I had an amazing family and a great support system that wanted to be there for me but I lived my life insecure and hiding what I was truly battling.

Part 3

The Reconciliation: Same Box, New Power

Box Shaking

I decided to participate in Princeton's nine-month service-learning program in large part to take a break from being in an intense academic environment so that I could grow emotionally, spiritually, and mentally. I wanted to be holistically healthy and I thought the year would give me the opportunity for personal growth I felt like I never had the time for in high school. The year exceeded my expectations in providing the space for self-growth, but I could never have anticipated how deeply God would challenge me through the experience. In Senegal, both having to learn new languages (Wolof and French) and battling social anxiety, I struggled to engage in the simplest social interactions. I even had a hard time using the bathroom because it was custom to use water instead of toilet paper. These more practical challenges were extremely humbling. In essence, I was a child again—I had to relearn the most basic aspects of life. The year provided a lot of space for reflection and many opportunities to be challenged. The combination of challenge and introspection led me to question more and more what I knew to be true about my life. Conversations with others from my Muslim instructor to my atheist peers led me to intentionally reflect on much of what I believed to be true. The daily necessity of having to humble myself to learn how to use the bathroom expanded into me humbling myself in all aspects of what I *thought* I knew about the world.

I began questioning myself and the world around me, every day. Moving from a predominantly Christian country to a Muslim one, I began to wonder what it really meant to be "Christian" in the first place. In addition to this, I was no longer living with Americans. The seven members of my bridge year cohort came from five different countries: the United States, Colombia, Mexico, Japan, and Wales. Now exposed to different cultural views, I began to identify and challenge my American values. Before coming to Senegal, I never consciously claimed an American identity. I saw myself as Black, but not necessarily as American. As an American, Senegalese people would constantly refer to me as a white person because of the privilege associated with being American. I began to ask myself, what does it mean to be American? What does it mean to be Black? What does it mean to be Christian?

Over the months, these questions began to tear at the very fabric of my understanding of the identities I had claimed in my seventeen years of life. I struggled to reconcile them. I began to seriously question the authenticity of my faith—how is my life different from those of my atheist friends? I still listened to secular music. It seemed the only difference between us was the fact that I went to church on Sunday. Was it my decision to save myself until marriage or did I just choose it because the people around me said so? Back at home, Christianity was the norm. Being in a country where I was the religious minority led me to question many of my most basic beliefs.

Around half way into the program, I had a mental breakdown. Having the most foundational parts of my identity challenged and becoming increasingly conscious of the experiences that shaped my life (the ones I share in this book), I felt paralyzed. I had already experienced the emptiness of my Princeton acceptance. Suddenly I found myself with what felt like no identity and an even deeper awareness of my lack of belonging. I began to feel like my very foundation had been ripped from under me. What value did

Christianity truly have in my life? It all seemed like a bunch of legalistic rules that kept me from doing what I wanted. Could my family have been wrong? Could all that I learned about how to exist in the world be wrong? Here no one cared that I was a PK. What was I to do? I had no one to seek approval from. No grades to validate who I was. No good deeds that people could applaud. No parents to tell me I was on the right track. Having all of these questions hit me at once was emotionally taxing. I was trying to hold onto what I knew while simultaneously learning new things. It seemed I was trying to use an old way of thinking to answer new questions and it just didn't work. Though I didn't fully realize it at the time, I needed God to bring light to what I was going through.

One day, I was with my Muslim instructor, Babacar Mbaye, and we began to discuss the goodness of God. At the conclusion of the conversation, he said, "what is the point of life if we don't have God? We worship the things God created and not the Creator." He paused; I paused. We both sat in silence. At that moment, a Bible verse I had always heard but never fully understood resonated deeply within me: "For what will it profit a man if he gains the whole world and forfeits his soul? Or what shall a man give in return for his soul?" (Matthew 16:26 ESV). This was one of the first times I was keenly aware that God was calling to me, speaking to me, and desiring to connect with me. I realized that while I had given my life to Christ nine years prior to this moment, I had allowed my soul to be tied to the world, to desire things that God created rather than the Creator himself.

This was a pivotal moment in my journey. Prior to then, I believed that I didn't need God to perform any miracles in my life. I mean, after all, I was going to Princeton, on the way to *grand* "success"—why would I need God to work in my life? It was from this moment onward that I would begin to more consciously wrestle with the experiences and beliefs that made up my life. I filled journal after journal with all of my thoughts, feelings, memories, convictions, and doubts. It was during this time that I remembered my suicide attempt and began to reflect on my decisions and my relationships with others, myself, academics, and God. I became extremely aware of how low my self-worth was, and how much I hated my body. I remember the moment I sat in my homestay mom's room journaling. I looked up at her and said, "I think I hate myself...I really hate myself." I knew I didn't like myself but prior to that moment, I had normalized all the negative feelings I felt. For the first time, it was like I could actually *see* how unhealthy my self-image was.

"Lan la?", "What do you mean?" my homestay mom inquired when she saw me talking to myself.

"Nothing, I'm just thinking," I responded in Wolof (the local Senegalese language).

I always had a habit of self-deprecation around my close peers. I couldn't accept that I was beautiful. While I once saw this as no big deal, I realized that it was my lack of self-esteem that led me to so easily get in a sexual relationship with that guy despite knowing God's standard for sexual purity. For the first time, I acknowledged that hating myself was doing a lot of damage in my life and I wanted to change. I had set out for freedom, and self-love seemed like the first place to start.

As I began to question and relearn, I ultimately had to choose to let go of preexisting beliefs—even the ones I would potentially reclaim. Not that I wouldn't pick them up again, but in order to fully take in all the new, and gain an authentic, fresh perspective, I had to create an intentional space between my old life and my present journey. Letting go of all of my notions of "good" and "bad." The process of letting go started small and evolved into letting go of my most basic truths. Did it matter that I had sex? What would happen if I did? I knew intellectually that sex created soul ties and distracted you from purpose but for so long I made the decision out of fear of instantaneous punishment from my dad and from God. My heart was so fear-driven, so suppressed, that I needed to let it all go. Was there a God? I felt that the answer was yes, but I needed to discover it for myself, not just believe it through the words of my parents. I had to let go in order to learn something new—to make sense of it all. In essence, I had to step out of the box that was my life up until that point and look at it from the outside. This was a scary, and yet liberating process. I identified what exactly was holding back. I became conscious of my chains. After all, one can't get free without identifying what is holding them back. I had to free myself from my limited perception of the inside walls and begin to see *all* of the box, *all* of me. I had set out to figure things out for myself no matter how intimidating it felt.

Problem Identified

I spent hour after hour, journal entry after journey entry, book after book, searching for answers. I read books and articles on anything from self-love to our need for significance to the impact of childhood trauma. I read endless articles on the importance of self-love and the importance of setting our own definitions and lifestyles. Not even fully understanding what it is I wanted to be free of, I just knew something - I wanted to be free and I didn't care at what cost. One of the first things that struck me about all that I had been through was the duality of the facades I worked to maintain. After all of my preaching on worthiness, I still went home with thoughts of suicide, imagining a better world where I was nonexistent. I would go home after preaching about freedom still bound to pornography. I continued to hate who I was and the body I had despite preaching body positivity. Every day, I would wake up and still be the same. Most days, I would feel like I had forgotten God or that He had forgotten me. I was saved, but I never asked God to save me from what I was struggling with. At the same time, I truly believed that I was okay. After becoming aware of the emptiness and bondage in my life, I couldn't help but ask, "How is it that someone who spent the majority of their time in church and participating in service projects is this depressed? How is it that I spent so much time giving while running on empty? How did I preach to people the joys of Christ, while accepting constant sin in my own life?" I confused God with religion; I thought the church *was* Jesus. I allowed myself to receive knowledge about Christ but I didn't know how to truly invite Him in to heal me and deliver me from my sin. I read the Bible to learn about God; I didn't know how to study the Bible in a way that taught me to give my pain and insecurity to God. My public actions may have created a facade of a "good Christian," but my heart, and my actions when people weren't around, were far from it in so many ways. Looking back, I believe keeping God in a box is what enabled me to make it to "the top" (Ivy league acceptance) and still feel empty. Essentially, I limited God to religion. I then used religion as a Pastor's Kid to seek validation for behaving a certain way. Church wasn't about being changed; it was part of a routine. The "God box" is what triggered all of my other vain attempts for validation, love, and joy in the midst of the hurt, despair, and emptiness that I worked so hard to suppress.

When my dad became a pastor and we moved to Morristown, NJ, I became more aware of my role as the pastor's daughter (PK). Realizing that the church had a predetermined way for me to behave, I began to conform to this role. I worked to appear as innocent as possible and supported this persona by doing well in school. This became a place of validation as the more I behaved by the "PK Standards," the more people would approve of me, and the better I felt about myself. Far from an intimate relationship with my Creator, I tried to use the regulation of religion as a means to achieve self-worth. The attempts failed miserably.

After taking the time to understand how I ended up where I was upon my Princeton acceptance, it seemed so obvious to me how these false sources of validation and identity were hurting me. I couldn't see it because I was moving so fast to reach my goals; I was running. I was constantly trying to prove myself. I wanted to be someone for somebody because the pain of not knowing who I was and not belonging hurt too much. The fear of having to confront what seemed impossible to heal drove me to distract myself with anything else: food, relationships, academics, pornography, you name it. I couldn't see that I was hurting. I was running so fast that not only was I not cognizant that I was being held back by all of these extra weights, but I also missed all the times God was begging me to let Him in. During all of this, I was preaching, I had Christian friends and we would discuss the importance of God, and I was sitting in church service after church service, all the while managing to keep God out of the most broken areas of my life.

Sunday after Sunday I would see people getting saved. I would see God performing miracles, and I would sing songs about God's strength and ability to save, yet I never believed that He was able to do more in my life because I didn't realize I needed Him too. I was preaching, yet simultaneously maintaining an ungodly relationship, perpetuating anger, living with unaddressed hurt from my childhood, and suffering from pornography addiction—these were all a testament to my inner contradictions that resulted in a deep emptiness. Something deep within me knew that what I was experiencing was less than what God had for me.

"God-boxing," confining God to my religious mindset, had me on a run, desperately searching for fulfillment, hoping that something would fill what I didn't know at the time, was a God-shaped hole in my heart. God was more than just a legalistic judge, He was a loving Father and friend and I simply did not know how to let Him in and heal what was broken. The ignorance of my identity in Christ and this God-shaped hole led to an escape from the realities of life, a misguided purpose, and a diminishing of my value in relationships.

My Blackness and femininity are essential parts of my identity, but they are not its essence. I tried to use my "Black woman" identity as my main source of worth, but it left many of life's questions unanswered and it didn't give me a profound, transcendental sense of purpose. Even more so, it was through this identity that I harbored more and more anger against social systems and more privileged people, and I took minimal time to care for myself. Anger kills the one who is bearing it most and my lack of self-care only exacerbated its effects on me. The anger I harbored made people afraid to have discussions and share what they were feeling with me. With white people, despite my best intentions, I actually widened the gap between us, making racial tensions even more pronounced. It was necessary for me to explore my Black identity, but it had begun to limit me because it could not speak to all of my complexities as a human being, as a child of God. It couldn't speak to the complexities of who I was as a material *and* spiritual being created for an intimate relationship with my Heavenly Father.

While I am a Black woman, I am simultaneously not that alone, because "Black woman" is a simplification of my identity and experiences. In the way that I was living, it forced me to put the other parts of my identity second. Being able to establish my transcendent identity in God first, however, enabled me to face the realities of what it meant to be Black, without feeling like I had to be boxed into that reality. I could look at white people differently. I recognized that there are social systems that are involved in the very racist realities of America and therefore I ought to give white people grace. The fact that many white people live in fear and spend so much time hating others inhibits them from fully living life. In effect, their whiteness, even though they are afforded privileges, also puts limitations on their human expression as children of God created in His image. I could not come to this realization until I stepped out of my "Black woman" box and allowed God to give me His heart for racial reconciliation. I had to step out of all the limited perspectives of the world in order to see the pain that racism can also cause white people. I am in no way diminishing what Black people have gone through, the importance of knowing Black history, or the importance of Black identity, but the moment that that identity becomes greater than God, it has the potential to do so much more harm than good. It was within the process of reclaiming my Black identity that I felt justified in hurting other people. Once I recognized and believed that I was a child of God first, I was empowered to love others unconditionally with God's heart as He gave me the ability.

On the surface, I really was fighting for racial equality, but there was an underlying plea in all of my arguments. It was as if every "Black lives matter" proclamation was a cry, attempting to affirm my own existence. It's as if I was trying to convince myself that Black lives really did matter, that *I* mattered. I clung to my heritage, history, and culture because it was all that I had to affirm my identity. I felt like I was drowning in a sea of white and in all of my social activism, I truly desired to be heard above all else. I had so much self-hatred, that I didn't truly believe that I mattered. My Black power persona gave me importance, but whenever I would take the mask off, I was left with just me. "Black Nicole" was a way that I could fight for my existence and affirm my life experiences. I was fighting for existence in the social context of racial oppression. My identity was established within the context of an oppressive system, rather than something transcendental and completely separate from world systems. Because I did not know myself more holistically, any threat to my Black identity was a threat to who I was as a person.

My life was a cycle of running from my hurt and running to what I thought would give me fulfillment. The world presents so many falsities of what a "good life" is. I was seeing other people's external features, believing that if I did what they did, I could also *look* the way they did or have the things they had. I saw Black women with natural hair, saw their contentment with who they were, and thought that if I had natural hair, I could be happy. I saw Black activists fighting for the cause of racial justice and finding a deep sense of purpose in that so I thought in my fight for racial justice, I would also find a deep sense of purpose to direct the rest of my life. Just as I worked to find purpose and identity as a Black woman, which presented its own set of limitations and burdens in my life, my goal of attaining an Ivy League acceptance also failed to fulfill me. I was looking at people with Ivy League degrees, seeing their success and what I thought was happiness, and so I thought that if I could attain this, I would also be happy. I had this false purpose that I thought, with college acceptance, would *finally* fill that God-shaped hole. I was trying to attain the mirages of what a good life looks like. I was looking on the outside and trying to maintain the end goal, without looking at peoples' inside and what constituted that. This ultimately led to an internal death. An inner life filled with shame, insecurity, anxiety, fear, and depression. On the outside, I was doing well because I was on the track to attaining all the things that constituted a "good life," meanwhile I was spiraling, feeling more and more empty.

I had no idea that the all-powerful God wanted me to remain pure because He cared about me. Religion always seemed like a bunch of rules to follow, something you do to stay good in God's eyes, something that restricted freedom and human expression. Being so empty, I used pornography as an escape from reality at the expense of my holiness in God's eyes. In the midst of my race for fulfillment, I needed something to deal with my day-to-day dissatisfaction with life. Pornography became my primary source of escapism. The problem with my escapism is that it worsened my insecurities, made me feel emptier, and my problems would still be there afterward. My dissatisfaction with life manifested in my anger with other people. Pornography didn't bring any solution to my situation and the joy I got from it was fleeting. I fell into a cycle of emptiness in which attempts for temporary escape through work, relationships, or porn would leave me feeling more empty.

My pornography addiction arose from my curiosity about sex, I never intended to be addicted but because sex remains a taboo topic, I never received biblical teaching on sex. One could blame this on my parents, but I don't, and I think it would be too easy to do so. I believe the church as a whole needs to do a better job. Not only did I put God in a box in my own life, but religion also puts God in a box. Sex is something created by God; it shouldn't be stigmatized. Sexual desire is something created by God; porn should not be a taboo topic. If we believe in a God that is above everything, then there should be nothing that we are too afraid to discuss within the church. We should be having open and honest conversations so that we can be free from the things that are silently killing us. It was religion's habit of putting God in a box that reinforced my own efforts in doing so.

In the midst of all the love I received from friends and family, I somehow manipulated it to speak to all of my insecurities and self-hatred. Having had a secret pornography addiction for so long, I had developed many sexual desires that would play out in my mind even though I never acted on them. I never thought I would. The rule of sexual purity was one that I would vow to never break, at least in my actions. Of course, there is more love than just self-love and a man's love but I never realized this or took the time to think about it. I hated myself so intensely that I sought love in relationships with men. There is God's love that was displayed through the words and actions of family and friends but not knowing about the profoundness nor the practicalities of His love, I finally fell doing the one thing I thought I would *never* do. I needed validation through relationships because I didn't value myself and I would consume myself in a relationship so that I could find that validation. It started in my attempts at friendship and became so intense that I sought it in a sexual relationship. I was looking for someone to affirm my existence, to see me as intelligent and beautiful, because I couldn't believe it myself. God's message of love and affirmation of my identity, I would twist to feed into my insecurity and self-hatred. Someone would say, "You're beautiful", and I would think, "They don't really mean it." Someone would say, "You are so smart," and I would think, "not smart enough though."

Dissatisfied with life and with who I was, I was always diminishing my own value whether it was in the way that I talked and treated myself or in my relationships with others. Unhealthy relationships ultimately came out of my own misunderstanding of who I was, and thus, I let people into my life whom God never intended for me to have relationships with. I diminished my own value so much so that while God declared my body a temple, I used it to feel the love that He had already given me in excess. I had phenomenal friends and yet because I was trying to get them to fill a God-shaped hole in my life, no matter what they did, I was always unsatisfied.

We all have an innate desire to be loved. God created us for it. He created us to be in community; he created us to feel valued;

he created us to both receive and give love. But why is it that so many of our attempts to find love leave us more hurt and feeling less lovable? Despite having parents who loved me, friends who cared about me, and an entire church community praying for me, I did not feel loved—I couldn't receive it. When someone gave me a compliment, I would cringe. When people called me beautiful, I would cringe. When people said I was smart, I would say they were lying. If someone tried to show me love I would reject it because I felt like I didn't deserve it. So caught up in what I thought I needed, I couldn't be joyful with the amazing people I had in my life. I was stuck in cycles of validation-seeking, anger, and false purpose that were sucking all the joy out of my life. But one encounter with God was going to change all of that.

New Identity

During my gap year, I got close to one of my Princeton peers in the program, Isabel. She and I found ourselves in similar situations. We were raised in the church and knew God was important, yet we were consumed and constantly burned out by the demands of school and our passion for social activism. God just didn't fit into our schedules. Because I felt so incredibly depressed after getting into Princeton, I decided to begin a daily devotional as a means to get closer to God. The first three days of the devotional were about the final return of Christ. At the same time that I was doing the devotional, Isabel was also seeing many signs in her life connected with this theme of the return of Christ. We both took this as a serious sign that we needed to start taking God more seriously.

As I began the devotional, I felt led to join a bible study on discerning God's voice. Isabel agreed to do it with me. During this study, I learned that willing obedience was the key to how we become able to discern the voice of God. The Bible study leader blatantly asked us if we truly wanted to discern God's will. If so, then we had to surrender our ambitions and sacrifice our own will in exchange for His. I decided that I was done with my old ways and that I really did want His will for my life. The concept of obedience was hard for me to swallow because it had strong associations with punishment and legalism for me, but I learned that true obedience, the obedience that God intends for us, is not a list of dos and don'ts. Throughout the study, I learned about all the different ways God could speak to us. She said, "Our discernment will never be perfect but God is loving and patient, and as long as we are actively abiding in Him when we are wrong, He will correct us and put us on the right path." This was powerful for me. The idea of having an intimate relationship with the Creator of the Universe seemed too good to be true—it was too great for me to fathom. Whereas I would have once skipped bible study to meet other obligations, even when my schedule got busy, I kept going to the bible study. Session after session, I would learn more and more about who God was and what He could possibly want with someone like me.

One day, God said so clearly to me, "Nicole, I love you. I love you when you are deep in sin. My love never changes based on how you act. I just want what is best for you. Nicole, you are fearfully and wonderfully made in My image. I am Love. I love you. There is nothing you could do to make me stop loving you." He just kept saying my name and he kept saying how much he loved me. For weeks, He just kept speaking to me, kept calling me by name. He continued to confirm for me in various ways that He didn't want me to refrain from sin because He wanted me to be unhappy, but in actuality He wanted me to be free from sin so that I could live the most joyful life He had planned for me. For lack of a better word, I was shook. When I was alone in my room, I would get on my knees and just cry, overwhelmed by all of the revelations I was having in such a short period of time. I would wake up early in the morning, pray, and read the Bible for hours. In my free time, I would watch sermons. I watched about two to three hour-long sermons every day. God began to reveal Himself to me as I took the time to be with Him.

Realizing how much God loved me, I began to take everything

to Him. I was utterly honest with where I was. I brought to Him my ugliest, darkest, thoughts—the thoughts that I previously thought He would *never* accept. He said, "Nicole when you were sinning I was with you the whole time. I made you; I know you. I know your thoughts before you think them. I am not asking you to bring it to me so I'll know, I'm asking that you bring it to me so that *you* can be free from it." I went from having an every-now-and-then kind of prayer life to praying at least five times a day. Proverbs 3:5-6 became my life. "Trust in the Lord with all your heart, and do not lean on your own understanding. In all your ways acknowledge him, and he will make your paths straight." (ESV). I took the time to take everything to Him. Day by day, I would submit my will to His and ask Him to enter every part of my life that I knew was broken.

"I want to want you, but I just don't see your importance right now. Allow me to see your importance." My prayers started like this and got increasingly more transparent.

"Dear God, I don't want to hate people like Rachel."

"Dear God, me again, I want to appreciate my friends but I don't. Help me value them for who they are."

"Lord God, when I look at myself, at my body, I am not happy. I want to be happy but I can't help but point out the things that are wrong with me, and even the things I perceive that are right about me I only perceive as right because of my social conditioning. I don't want to hate myself anymore. I know you say that I am fearfully and wonderfully made, but I don't believe it. I want to be at peace with it; I want to love it the way that you do. Help me to love myself, please. As long as I continue to have low self-worth, the easier it will be for me to give my body away. Lord God, have my heart. I don't want to be tied or dependent on anything or anyone but You."

God can't bless us where we pretend to be. He can only bless us where we really are. I had to get very serious with God about where I really was. I couldn't put up facades anymore. It was hard, but I had begun to lay the foundations of a relationship with God. I was now abiding in God. It was the beginning of an intentional, joy-filled life, where I could have peace that would surpass all human understanding. I knew clearly who was fighting for me, and repenting of all my sins enabled me to live in my most authentic light. I was still dealing with the thoughts, actions, and pain of my past life, but I could now truly grow into who God created me to be. In fact, God used the darkest parts of me to be the primary ingredient for growth. My pain provided a perfect place for God to work in me. I still didn't fully know how new life would turn out, but the process of giving everything to Him allowed Him to lay a foundation and build from the ground up. While I couldn't see it right away, I knew the seeds He was planting in me would eventually grow into fruit. I knew I would soon reap the harvest of this new commitment to my relationship with God.

Every day we have two choices: to be empty or to fight, to be barren or to battle. Some of us consciously enter the battle determined to win; others consciously go into the battle but get weighed down and become defeated. Many of us have no idea there is even a battle to fight at all—and before we even think to pick up our boxing gloves, we just accept the barrenness. Thinking that this is the only way to live, we learn to manage life in the emptiness, the abyss, and the darkness. We distract ourselves as a means to forget that we are in the darkness. In my revived walk with God, I was no longer barren, but this simultaneously meant that I now had to fight to maintain the fruit that God was growing in me.

As I moved forward in Christ, I would be reminded of my past mistakes. The devil kept trying to plant seeds of hopelessness; he worked hard to try and bring me back to my former barrenness. I was now entering a new way of life and the only way for me to keep moving forward was to have the courage to do so. The relationship I was building with God was so precious to me that I was willing to give up anything to maintain it. I now had to have the courage every day to walk out in faith. I had to have the courage to start cutting out old habits. While painful, I had to end relationships with people who were tempting me to do the wrong thing; I had to spend less time talking about issues and spend more time in prayer.

Just because I gave it to God, didn't mean that I was free from problems—in fact, it seemed as if the problems became stronger and more apparent. The memories of pain and hurt would resurface again and again, but I kept giving them to God. I recognized that the power ultimately arose from my response. Would I go back to my old life, or would I keep moving forward? Despite how I felt, I continued to praise God and abide in Him. All these things kept happening, and I had to choose. Would I dwell on the pain or would I dwell on His goodness? Did I really mean it when I said I wanted to solely serve the Lord? As I continued to reflect on my life experiences, I would keep taking it to God. I decided that I would never have lukewarm faith again.

Sometimes I would just have to tell my emotions to shut up and praise the Lord. As hard as it was, I decided that my ultimate response would be to bless the Lord at all times. I would meditate on Who was on my side and be at peace. If God was for me then literally no one, not even my experiences and unhealthy relationships, could block me from my purpose. I said to myself, "I may have experienced emotional abuse as a child that has left me wounded; I may have low self-esteem; I may have carried generational curses and burdens from my parents and their ancestors; I may not be where I want to be currently in life, but my God is greater. I am not dismissing the pain. I am wounded. I am angry. I am hurting. I am tempted to go back to pornography again. I do want to yell at this racist person. But I am praising God for all that He has done and all that He continues to do—all that He is, and that He has been, and all that He will be because I serve an unchanging God. My pain is worthy of acknowledgment, worthy of healing, worthy of time, worth sharing, and I know God will take care of it." I would memorize scripture and recite it so that it would be "hidden in my heart" (Psalm 119:11). I became increasingly comfortable with not having the answers because I knew that God had them. I simply maintained the courage and faith to keep walking with Him; I knew He would work everything out.

———————•———————

One Sunday at church during my gap year, after a long week of feeling defeated, I remembered a moment of inexplicable joy. I didn't want to go to church that day, but I went anyway because I knew God was the only reason I was still living. Exhausted, I pressed through praise and worship anyway. As I sang along with the choir, I began to feel a deep sense of warmth, joy, comfort, and safety. I remembered the deep transcendental joy I felt that day I got saved ten years prior and felt as if I was being filled with that joy all over again. I had, what I can articulate now to be, a direct encounter with my Heavenly Father. I began to cry. I thought, "I actually *want* to live." I hadn't even realized it, but I had never actually dealt with all the pain I felt when I attempted suicide. I just got wrapped in sin and a misguided pursuit of purpose. I hadn't realized that for years I was living with no real desire to live. Now, the thought of the future made me excited.

Over the next couple of weeks after that Sunday, God began to remind me of the dreams I once had but had let go of for one reason or another. He reminded me of the book I wanted to write but had let go of. He reminded me of my efforts to lose weight that I kept giving up on. He reminded me that I used to want to be fluent in French. God told me, "Whatever you want, I'll give it to you. What do you want?" *What did I want?* When he first asked, I didn't know. I had become so used to just passively accepting life, that the idea of having my own vision was so new to me. But as I began to search my heart, He revealed a *new* vision for my life. I would get married one day to someone also abiding in God and fulfilling their purpose. The book that I was writing then, wouldn't be my last. One day, I would preach and teach to believers and non-believers alike; I would get to represent

Christ. I would be able to fully and completely walk in the fruits of the Spirit. I would have a godly community of friends supporting me.

While God had allowed me to remember the pain of my past, He also enabled me to remember the joy of my present and future in Christ. He even slowly began to change my desires. With this desire to live, my desire to watch pornography slowly died. The images would still come to my memory every now and then, but they weren't triggers to watch porn; they became triggers to pray and give it to God. My passion for singing, something I loved to do as a child, came back. Church used to be a place of stress, but now it was a place of transcendental joy. Experiencing this profound love and slowly becoming freed from the burden of my past, life truly felt like the greatest gift of all. I felt revived. I felt restored. Everything *was* connected. I began to realize that everything in my childhood—even the suicide attempt—was directly connected to the bondage and vanity I lived in. All of my hurting was rooted in the fact that I had a minimal relationship with God outside of my Sunday morning God-box. Deeply aware of my brokenness and my need to heal, I knew that I needed help and the only place I could get it was God. And once I turned to Him, I saw that He was more than willing to give me that help. With that realization, I was ready to leave my past. I had rediscovered my freedom in Christ.

Reconciled Identity

My friend James used to always have these "big picture moments" when he would think about the greater meaning of life. We would talk and he would go, "Nicole I'm having a big picture moment" and then proceed to share what inspired him to zoom out from what he could see right now in his life and gain a greater understanding of his current situation. As I grew with God, I began to have more and more big-picture moments. I began to move out of the perspectives that were holding me back from seeing all of my beauty and potential. I learned who God really was according to His Word and not just what I heard in church. One of my greatest revelations was learning that God was a loving Father. Thus, God does not punish us, he disciplines us. It was often the consequences of the way I was living that caused me problems, not His punishment. When I realized that I was dealing with the consequences of holding a false identity, I began to change. I had to let Him in, but only God could free me from this bondage. I know I had my new identity in Christ, and all of my past identities, such as my racial identity. Did they connect? Could they be reconciled? Was I supposed to just forget my past? In the initial drafting of this book, I wrote about the deconstructing of our box. I thought that we had to break down the walls and define for ourselves who we are. I realized, though, that there are many parts of our identity that we cannot change or choose, like the color of our skin. To say we must deconstruct the box and define ourselves diminishes the influence of our external environment on our identity. Therefore it is not that we must deconstruct the box, but rather reframe it. We have the ability to move inside and outside of the box (and not be limited by it), reorganize, repaint, to take control of what our box looks like inside and out.

I developed an identity in Christ and a love for God that gave me the power to change the way I viewed both myself and my experiences. As I reexamined my past and who I was, I simultaneously embraced a new and greater identity, I was then able to reframe the very experiences that were a source of pain. Did the fights with dad really mean that love was conditional? Did it really mean that I had to perform in order to get a man's love? Did my experiences with girls in school really mean I wasn't good enough? Why am I presently walking in the insecurity from 5 years ago? Were there other ways to experience love outside of porn and men? Was there another way to live as a Black woman other than denying my white family and living in anger?

For so long I was allowing my past to determine how I behaved in my present. I was consumed by self-hatred and insecurity that had started when I was twelve years old. There were scales on my eyes that prevented me from seeing the unlimited potential of myself and my future. I could only see the inside of my box when there was an entire outside waiting to be decorated. Now with God, I had begun to learn and walk in His promises and see a bright future in every aspect of my life.

My dad really only wanted to protect me. His efforts to discipline me were attempts to make me feel safe. I no longer had to fear my dad; he loved me. He didn't hate me; he wanted the best for me. He wasn't perfect, and I needed to stop living as if he should be. I had to stop living for his approval, and above all, I had to forgive him for the hurt he caused me. I had to let go of the resentment that I held against him and I wanted more than anything to let go of it because it was hurting me and preventing me from having a truly authentic and peaceful relationship with him and with others. I forgave my dad for his mistakes and also chose to recognize all of the positive elements that he fed into my life. Today, I am so grateful for the way he raised me. I wrote a letter to my dad expressing my gratitude:

I don't nearly say it enough, but I love you, I value you, and I think you are the best dad I could have ever asked for and I'm not just saying that because I didn't have a choice in who my father was. You sacrificed so much in your life to ensure that my siblings and I could have opportunities that you were not afforded. As a child, I know that there is so much more you have done for me that you didn't share with me because that's just the type of superhero dad you are. I know whenever you lecture me, you think I am not listening but a lot of the time I am. Even if I disagree at the moment, I value what you say. You are so wise and I have learned so much from you. So many of the lessons I've learned, I have internalized to the point where I just see them as fact.

I forgive you for the emotional abuse you have caused me. I recognize that it has affected me in more ways than I thought. I am letting go. I am letting go of the pain and anger. I choose to love.

Maybe I am getting this all wrong. I recognize we all write different narratives in our heads as children. I had a naive perception of my experiences at the time but all emotions are valid, and I found it necessary to write this so you can understand how I have felt and do feel. I hope to initiate an open line of communication for us to discuss and grow together.

Thank you for raising me and teaching me, even when I didn't want to be educated, and I didn't even realize what you were showing me.

My dad responded to this letter with great gratitude and encouraged me to continue to bring my challenges to My Heavenly Dad. Through many honest, and at times painful conversations, therapy sessions, and a lot of patience and forgiveness, God has radically healed my relationship with my father over time.

My dad was the first, but not the last person with whom the Holy Spirit led me to reconcile. As it turns out, those girls from elementary school did not actually hate me. At my high school graduation, many classmates told me that they thought I didn't want to be their friend because I was so quiet. I had created a false narrative in my mind that nobody wanted to be my friend. In reality, people had their own fears and misperceptions about approaching me just like I feared pursuing them. I had also created false narratives about romance. I thought I could fill my need for love through a guy even if I did not know how to love myself. Blinded by that belief, I had developed a soul tie (an emotional connection) with someone who did not have my best interest at heart and it distracted me from my walk with God. Being dependent on another person for validation was only hurting me. I felt empowered to move forward in forming healthier relationships with others as God led me to reconcile with those from my past.

In addition to relational healing, God empowered me to let go of limiting beliefs around my racial identity. Why did I feel as if I had to choose between my racial identities? Why couldn't I accept the complexity of my identity, as Rachel did? What if I decided to let go of my preconceived notions of Blackness? What if I didn't hate myself for my whiteness? What if I stopped living out of my need to prove something? As I had begun to reexamine my Black identity, I reframed those Christmas Eve dinners. I could be Black and related to white people. My association with white culture did not invalidate my Blackness. Blackness is a spectrum of complicated people—yes linked by a history of oppression—but human beings first. I tried to fit into what I thought was the "right way to be Black," but there was no right way. Simply living, in my Black skin, in a way *that is authentic to me*, is Black life—no one could tell me that my unique expression of Blackness is wrong. As I lived in Senegal during my gap year, Blackness became increasingly normalized for me. Blackness began to feel uncomplicated. In Senegal, I still felt controlled by the gaze and opinions of my white peers. Would they affirm my existence or deny it? But this time, things were different. I was no longer in a world that told me my Black skin and my size were something to be despised. I was now in a world where Black bodies and larger frames were the norms. Yes, colorism was rampant in ads and women desired light skin, but Blackness was still the norm. My Blackness became normalized, and for once, whiteness became "the other." For once, I could walk down the street and see people that looked like me. I was now counting the number of white people I saw in a day. Granted, many people viewed me as a white person because of my American identity but I was being unconsciously affirmed in my existence as a Black woman by my environment every day.

There are parts of ourselves that we can't change, like the color of our skin or the family that we were born into, but we can change our perspective and the amount of control that we give those identities in our lives. Many of us live our lives from the inside of the box or try to maintain what someone else painted on the outside walls. We have the ability to paint our own box. We get to survey our walls, stare at our walls, and decide what is it we want to maintain, and what is it we desire to change. All of these realizations were simple, and when written, blatantly obvious, but I had been carrying so many false narratives, and I had never taken the time to reevaluate them. Even when I made friends in high school, and my relationship with my dad evolved, I would hold onto my fears and hurt from age eight or twelve years old. I needed to consciously reframe these experiences so I would no longer live in them subconsciously in my present.

Before I came alive in God, I didn't have my central identity founded in something transcendental, something that had no limitations on who I could be or what I could do, so I searched for an affirmation of my existence in the things and people in my life. The problem with this is that the validation they gave me was fleeting and usually caused more harm than good in the end. Because their validation was temporary, I desperately sought any new opportunity to gain validation. I found an affirmation of my existence through school, my Blackness, and my Pastor's Kid identity. I looked for a sense of purpose in each of these. In school, my purpose was to get into an Ivy League school. In my Blackness, my purpose was to fight for racial equality. With Sam, I sought to be loved. These were finite sources of validation and came with their own baggage. When school finished I was burnt out and left feeling empty. When I was fighting for racial equality, my self-worth hung on the strings of who I was able to convince that Black lives did matter. Each of these sources of identity and purpose left me more hurt and broken than when I entered them.

Initially looking back on all the bondage and mistakes I made in my life, I couldn't help but think, "How could you be so blind? How could you be so naive? How could you be so stupid?" But the reality is that my conditioning began at a very young age and I realized that it was the Holy Spirit bringing things to light. So many of my actions were a result of learned behaviors I developed as a child. Because I saw these behaviors and mindsets as normal, I didn't question them until the Holy Spirit began to expose the cycles.

Freedom to Choose

Being free to live the way that God has always intended for me to live meant that I was equally free from all of the habits of my past. I was now in a relationship with my Creator. I was free from the need to be perfect. I was free from reaching certain standards to feel good about myself, from the need for other people's approval and free from all of the boxes of identity. Above all, I was free from the oversimplification of my identity. What God gave me was greater than any one category or role, or even the combination of roles I had used to find meaning in my identity.

The following is a letter I felt the Holy Spirit leading me to write to my past self during the closing of my Bridge Year journey. I believe that it captures the essence of what it means for me to truly be free from the despair that I was in.

I know that you are woke and that you have been oh-so-socially active. I understand your heart is in the right place. I am so proud of what you have accomplished. But during your time here in Senegal, you are going to learn, in a not-so-easy way, that "wokeness" is not the goal. "Wokeness" is not where one finds fulfillment. If you are honest with yourself, it is your "wokeness" that made you bitter; it is your "wokeness" that further entrapped you into the boxes that you were so adamant about deconstructing. You are going to learn that anger only feeds into unjust systems.

> You are going to learn that you don't have to live in boxes; you don't have to live in a preexisting niche of identity. I know you won't believe this immediately, but there is a point of intersectionality in which you can think and live and breathe and be free;

it is the intersectionality that creates the ideas, that enables you to fulfill your purpose. Each one of them provides a lens to see the world, each of them contributes a way of thinking, and combining your unique experiences and identities enables you to be the most authentic you. All of those boxes of identity, whether you have perceived them as privileges or disadvantages, can come together to create your most authentic self. Those boxes aren't to be thrown away. You are Black and a woman and quirky and corny and intelligent and low-income, but you are also simultaneously none of those because those terms are oversimplifications of the Nicole that you are.

You do not have to be imprisoned by these boxes. They are a part of you, and they are essential to reaching your most authentic self but don't allow any of them to impose limitations on what you can do. For 17 years you tried to fit into all of these boxes to the best of your ability because you thought it was what you had to do to be happy. Sometimes you failed, sometimes you succeeded, and sometimes you just ended up hurting yourself and others, but in all of these efforts, you never honestly felt authentically you.

You wouldn't believe, and you probably won't even understand me when I say, that in the next seven months you will find a way of living and thinking and existing that is unique from anything you have ever known. You are beautiful because you have learned to exist fearfully and wonderfully the way God created you.

So, Nicole, I know you are woke, and I know you are smart, and I know you have self-doubt, and

I know sometimes you feel like you don't know who you are or who you are supposed to be, but it is only because you have tried to reduce your existence to boxes. You no longer have to try and live in boxes; you no longer have to feel uncomfortable; you no longer have to wear different masks depending on the validation you need that day. You can just be free. Be free, be free, be free! I am being so adamant about this because I know you are not strong enough to get here on your own; I know you need to be pushed. Bridge Year is not only going to challenge your worldview–but it will also challenge your very existence, and you are going to be the better for it.

When you die, you don't get to take your boxes on judgment day; it will just be you and your decisions, and then what will you say? Who will you say you were? What will you say you did? I hope that you will not say that you were Black or poor or Princeton educated or good or bad or whatever other simplification of the human experience you can come up with.

I hope you will say that you were human, that you lived to simply worship God, and that you did the best that you could for Him. My greatest prayer for you is that you do not let go of this Truth, that you meditate on it day in and day out because it is from this understanding that you will be able to do the most magnificent work God has called you to do. So, Nicole, as you experience Senegal as Fatou Diagne, as you receive revelation after revelation and grow, keep your mind open - but whatever you do - do not be entangled by the lies of boxes that held you down for so long. Never forget, you are not a product

of identities but rather a phenomenal creation from
the Creator.

It all comes down to this: everyone in life has the inalienable
right to choose what type of life they want to live. This is a choice.
The problem is that many of us just accept our conditioning rather
than consciously choosing what we want in life. It is our purpose in
life to worship God, our Creator—it can feel like a vague purpose
and I believe that God sets it up that way intentionally. Each of us
has a unique set of personality traits, gifts, and experiences that
come together to create something beautiful—something that can
ultimately give glory to Him and that we can find ultimate fulfillment
in. In coming into my purpose, God asked me to write this book,
but that does not mean everyone is going to write a book when they
come into purpose. Everyone's way of glorifying God is going to be
different—nobody but God can tell us how to fulfill our purpose.
But He loves us so much that He does not choose that life for us.
He gives us the *choice* to love Him. This is true love. I thought that
my purpose in life was to attain a certain degree and a certain way
of life, and that is what would give me fulfillment. I was wrong. It
was my conditioning that told me that an Ivy League degree would
make me happy. It was my conditioning as a Black woman that told
me I had to be anti-system and dedicate my life to social activism.
I falsely believed that "enlightenment" or "wokeness" was the goal;
that once I had "the truth" about the world, then I would be fulfilled
in life. But it was my "enlightenment" and "wokeness" that led me to
perpetuate division and hurt people like Rachel. I wasn't truly happy
hurting her; I just thought that that was how it had to be. Fulfilling
purpose is supposed to bring joy to you and light and love into the
world, not create more division and destruction. I thought that she
was an inevitable casualty if she refused to agree with the "truth" that
I was feeding her, but I couldn't be further from the truth. I spent so
much time trying to fight a system and, in this way, I inhibited my
club's movement for social justice and racial harmony. Seeing myself

as Black first put limitations on what I could do because white people were the "others." Before I even entered a conversation, I recognized their humanity second and what I assumed to be the "monolithic white experience" first.

It wasn't until I acknowledged how unhappy I was that I was able to be free. I had settled in life. I had convinced myself, after the Princeton acceptance, that that was it. I was successful. That, however, couldn't have been further from the truth. Doing a gap year was just the time and space I needed to begin to breathe, to really come to terms with where I was in life and where I was going. I realized that the moment we try to reduce the complexity of our humanity to a set of identities is the moment we cease to be fully human. I kept trying to fit into preexisting niches of identity and they left me either hurt or empty because I was never made to fit those boxes! It's as if I kept trying to fit my uniquely shaped soul into these perfectly carved, squared boxes and I kept damaging parts of myself so that I could fit into those boxes. In reality, my soul has a unique shape from anyone that has lived or will ever live. I finally worked up the courage and faith to say, "No more. I am done trying to fit into boxes." At first, it was weird because everyone else seemed to be fitting into their boxes just fine. When you aren't adhering to the norm, your growth process looks really different from everyone else's. When I finally stopped trying to fit into societal standards, I confused people. They genuinely did not understand me. But I decided that what God says about me is greater than what any individual could ever say about me. What God tells me to do, is greater than what any person could have me do. And when I finally see my Lord on Judgment Day, I hope that he will look at my uniquely shaped and matured soul and say, "Well done, good and faithful servant" (Matthew 25:21 ESV).

Reframing how I perceived myself has enabled me to reframe my goals, and how I wanted to interact with those around me. I even reframed my sexuality for myself. I no longer lived by the fears of what my dad might say. I made decisions that I knew would be good for me as I weighed them against God's word. A once stigmatized, predetermined part of my life, I got to reframe and define for myself. I stopped watching pornography because it distorted my self-image and view of sex in general. Seeing women objectified for so long still makes it challenging to see through a pure lens, as I internalized these images. I had to learn that sex and sexuality are good things and nothing to be ashamed of; God puts these desires in me for a reason. It is the perversion of that desire that is dangerous. Pornography gave me a false sense of comfort, pleasure, and freedom because it was always available, but at the end of the day, it left me addicted, ashamed, and guilty. I chose, and still choose, to remain abstinent until marriage because I have found deep joy in my singleness. Living completely unattached from another person gives me the freedom to pursue God's purpose for my life. I choose purity because I desire it, not out of fear of the consequences of living an impure life. No longer afraid of punishment, I began to ask the greater question: What is beneficial? Pornography simply was not beneficial for me; it was draining.

Being free, I was able to set my own boundaries. I made the conscious decision to say no to society's conditioning. Society's standards prevented me from freedom. We have to choose to be free from this bondage. No more compromising who we are and our potential. Because of my new identity in Christ, I was given the strength to say, "No," to the bondage of my past. I was so blinded by what I thought I had to be, so caught up in trying to suppress all of the "wrong" in me, that it was stealing all of my joy. It was a conscious decision to say, you *can't* hold me in these chains anymore. I began to walk in hope for the future and not fear of the past. I used to live in fear that I was unlovable, now I live in the knowledge that I am loved by the Creator of the Universe—each identity and every one of my experiences fitting into God's perfect plan for my life.

Loving People

What are the implications and the fruits of my journey beyond my own personal growth? Why is it so important that we become free? Why is it so important that we learn to fight? If we do not know who we are, we cannot walk in our purpose. If we are not walking in purpose, we are not reaching our full potential as human beings or impacting others the way we were meant to. When I came to Senegal, my dad reminded me that being myself is the best gift I could give to those around me. While initially, I didn't understand the significance of this advice, I realize now that before trying to build relationships with others, I needed to build a relationship with the One that truly matters first. God calls us to be the lights of the world, meaning that *as we shine,* people will be attracted to us and also want to experience the joy that we experience in shining. When we learn how to fight the battle for ourselves, we can begin to help other people fight their battles. We can give them tools and encouragement.

Having learned about myself, I am able to be more compassionate with others and their situations. Knowing that my identity and purpose were secured in Christ, I was able to reach out to others. I am in a better position to give and be in relationships with other people. The better I get at understanding myself: how I love, how I hurt, and who I am, the better I can understand and empathize with these things in other people.

My ability to love Rachel is a primary example of this. My love for her went from zero to infinite because I was more aware of what God has done and continues to do for me. Knowing the depths to which God loved me, I willingly loved other people. Not to say that it wasn't difficult, but God had been too good to me for me to actively hurt one of His children. I made efforts to apologize to everyone I had hurt in my life. I explained that I was hurting, and had a lot of wounds that needed healing, and I wasn't dealing with the pain the right way. Rather than looking inward, I projected my pain outwardly onto other people.

Even more so, I recognized that Rachel specifically was never my enemy—in fact, she was also a victim of a system designed to keep us all in boxes, designed to keep us from loving each other. I began to recognize that the war I was fighting was between the stronghold of racism in my mind and on this earth, not against any person. We are all just living in the ways that we were conditioned to until we learn to do better, and none of us can be blamed for that. Identifying people as "problems" drives us further apart and takes us even further away from a solution. We need to love each other in a way that is so deep that we will want to be vulnerable and we will want to be free.

When we are walking with our God-given identity and, in our God-given purpose, we interact in relationships in ways that will glorify God. We cannot encourage individuality in relationships if we do not first know ourselves. When we enter relationships with people who don't know themselves, we can hurt them unintentionally. Two people coming together, without identity and without a clear purpose, and with no direct aim within the relationship, is a recipe for disaster. Thus, a lack of identity makes healthy relationships literally impossible.

Once I discovered who I was in Christ and began walking in purpose, I interacted in relationships in a way that encouraged individuality. Being free from the opinions of others, I was able to have friendships with people, believers and nonbelievers alike, who were supporting my walk with Christ.

———— • ————

Not only was I better able to love others, but I also began to see love as the solution to much of the division in our society. My inner work was not only the foundation to my relationships, but it also laid the foundation for how I interact with the problems of the world and our communities. We must learn to live in harmony with our own contradictions before we can even begin to understand the complexity of others, nonetheless the vast complexity of larger systems.

Today I recognize that genuine relationships are how we can move past the divisions of racism. Obviously, structural racism is very real and there must be policy in place and activists fighting for that policy for our system to change. But when it comes to the day-to-day dealing with racial tension, we will not move past it until we learn to love each other for the human beings that we are. Before I am Black, I am human. Before any white person is white, they are human. If we are both human, then we both cry, we both love, and we both want peace. We have the same capacity for emotion and desire and aspirations for a good life. It is from this common ground that we can move forward in love and in unity. Racism, like all of the problems of today, is a result of complex human beings just like us. Everything is more complicated than it seems, and it takes communication skills, patience, and love to understand everyone's perspectives before we place blame on anyone. True community is founded on healthy relationships because it is in these relationships that we can build bridges for a community whose foundation is based on reconciliation.

I believe that what our society lacks is true understanding because (1) we don't know how to listen—instead, we have been conditioned to produce answers, and (2) we don't allow for authentic relationships because we are afraid of the vulnerability that they require. I believe that having the vulnerability to say we don't know is the foundation for creating long-term, sustainable solutions to all of the issues we face today. As long as we continue to make assumptions about the "other," as long as we hold anger and bitterness, as long as we pretend and wear facades, the longer we will perpetuate hurt and suffering. Vulnerability is not easy, but it is the cornerstone of healing. Until we learn to listen, develop relationships, and be vulnerable, we will keep hurting ourselves, each other, and the planet, and ultimately will perpetuate oppressive systems of inequality.

I still believe in the power of activism, but I no longer see it solely as a means to reach some tangible end goal. The fight is for freedom. The freedom of Blacks and Whites and all colors alike. Genuine efforts toward racial harmony are to be founded on the recognition of each person's humanity. I have developed *relationships* with the people around me that make me *want* to help. I do not want to serve others because I think I can fix all problems, but simply because I am invested in people's lives. I know that what I offer is little. In fact, it adds up to nothing compared to what people have done for me in my life, but giving is about reciprocity. I give what I can, and that is all I can do, and whatever I do, it is out of genuine love for people.

We are all called to be a part of the beloved community. We each have a unique set of gifts and experiences that God desires to get the glory from. As we get to more deeply understand ourselves, we develop a deeper understanding of the world around us and how we're connected to it. We are able to identify the areas we are called to be a part of and where we are meant to have a positive impact. Rather than trying to fit in where we perceive there is a need, we can live the most impactful lives from our own authentic passions. If you're like me, you may not even be fully sure of what you want in life or how you'll go about getting it, but I am a sure believer that when we put God first and trust Him with our desires, He will surely make a way out of no way and do exceedingly and abundantly more than we could ever ask or imagine (Psalm 37:4; Ephesians 3:20-21). The deep healing work He does inside of us will ripple out and allow us to walk in purpose in our relationships with other people and in our communities at large.

Conclusion

Today I am unapologetically on my journey of obtaining my Ph.D. in Sociology and pursuing my calling to entrepreneurship in the online business space. Pursuing my dreams and living out my God-given purpose would never have been possible without this "unboxing" revelation the Lord gave me. Today, it is the basis for my life and business coaching programs. I encourage you to take heart and know that when you realize that God has more for you than what this world has to offer you, you will find yourself with joy and freedom you never thought possible.

The box is a gift that each of us receives from God—it is our talents, our desires, our dreams, our identities, our ambitions, our soul, our spirit, and our body. The ability to unbox all that we are is a gift from God rooted in His love for us. When God gives us this box, it is up to us to open it, enjoy it, and make the most of what we are given. Even though we are the only ones with the power to open it, many of us let the world control it. We are afraid of who we might become when we open it or how those around us may react to what's inside, so we keep it closed. We let the world write on our walls. We let those around us put labels and identities on us. We let the world tell us who we must be and how we must behave. We live insecure lives, constantly seeking approval from others—not even realizing that the approval we are searching for can only come from God. Meanwhile, our gifts and dreams stay in the dark, wasting away inside the box like precious jewels in a forgotten storage unit. So desperate for acceptance and love from those around us, we think we'll be happier if we hide and be what other people tell us to be or do what everyone else around us is doing. We go through life as victims of our own experiences, both the good and the bad ones. We allow our experiences to define us. As this happens, many of us become bitter and resentful towards those around us who shaped our experiences for the worst. We blame other people for our unhappiness, but the truth is (as cliché as it sounds): *our joy doesn't come from the people around us; it comes from within.*

My life is a prime example of this pattern. I had so much love and support throughout my life. I have three siblings who love me dearly, parents who have supported me through nearly every single one of my decisions, and extended family who have gone out of their way to ensure I've always had what I needed. Even in the midst of feeling lost in my adolescence, I still had found a sense of fulfillment in learning and purpose in my heart for social justice. My life was good and truly blessed. Yet, internally, I was still struggling because I didn't know how to make sense of who I was and my life experiences. I lived in fear of rejection, desperate to be loved and accepted. I was insecure so I held onto every form of validation to make me feel significant. I didn't know who I was, so I sought identity through being a "pure" Pastor's Kid and a "woke" Black woman. I tried to use both of these incomplete identities to meet my needs for significance, love, and security. I worked to live up to others' preconceived notions about my identity because I thought I was supposed to. I always felt stuck between the intersections of various influences. On one hand, I didn't know who I was—as a person, as a child of God, as a Black woman, and, more recently, as a Princeton student. I didn't understand how all of these things came together; I didn't know that reconciling these pieces of myself was possible. I felt myself hopping between these identities depending on who I was with. This inner struggle, combined with the insecurity that every teenage girl has, the anxiety I experienced when changing schools, and the lack of affection I felt from my dad–all led to inner paralysis. I felt like I just had to accept the confusion and live in this seemingly irreconcilable tension. I suffered in silence because I had no idea there was another way of living. What I thought I had to passively accept as my life was really my own warped perspective of my reality.

At the end of the day, I was my own oppressor. I was the only one limiting myself. It was I who allowed these labels to be the sources of my value. After having a radical encounter with God's love, I began to search for a better way to live. With God's guidance, I began this process of unboxing which freed me to explore the intersectionality of my identities, experiences, and gifts. When I traded striving for perfection for resting in God's love, I found inexplicable freedom. In this freedom, I am able to become the best version of myself and live my most fulfilled life. Simply put, I don't have to pretend anymore. My worth is no longer in what I do but in who I am: I am a child of God. The unboxing has given me the freedom to explore my various gifts, talents, and desires that I hid out of fear of rejection, and because I thought they didn't fit with who I was expected to be. Shut inside the box, I was a victim of my experiences and who people said I had to be. On the outside of the box, I got to choose how my experiences would (or wouldn't) define me.

Society told me that based on what I had accomplished by getting into Princeton, I had succeeded, but I couldn't settle for that. I couldn't accept the idea that I had "arrived," because there was so much more that I wanted to do and be, and at the same time there was still so much pain I didn't know how to articulate. I've learned through my journey that acknowledging the pain is not disregarding the joy I did have. I believe God simply wanted me to have more. The suicide attempt, the academic strivings, and the failed relationships were all experiences and habits that I didn't realize were doing more harm than I thought. Since embarking on this journey, I have become far more self-aware and self-compassionate. I have learned to love myself. This self-awareness has helped me make better decisions. I am progressing. I am becoming. And now, having been reconciled, I can begin to forge my own path. I no longer walk boxed into the confines of four walls. I walk in grace; I have freedom. I am free from being blindly drained. I do not say I have freedom to say that I won't ever be hurt again, that I won't make mistakes again, or that I will never have moments of blindness again. Rather, this freedom is an awareness of who I am. It is the freedom to understand *why* I do the things that I do and feel the things that I feel.

The process of unboxing has required that I make the conscious choice every day to live in freedom, authentic to who I am and not by the waves of culture and the people around me. Every day, I make decisions based on my values and my dreams. Making decisions out of my authenticity does not guarantee that I always make the right decision, but it does mean that I can learn from them. Each decision is an opportunity for me to learn more about myself and what I value. They are decisions I am making for myself, not for other people. I am proud of every single one of my decisions because they are coming from an authentic version of myself, rather than the surface levels of identity I once held on to. I am no longer striving for some arbitrary standard of perfection; I am committed to becoming the best version of myself.

When I imagined writing a book, I never thought that *this* would be it. Surely, I thought I would write about race relations or the college process––things that were very close to my heart and that I put a majority of my time into. I thought I'd write about a topic where I had it all together, rather than open up about my deepest struggles, but God has a way of messing up our plans and putting us on better paths we never imagined. This book for me is the path of discovering unexpected power in vulnerability. Many of us are looking for perfect or incredibly successful people to look up to. When I told one of my sisters about many of my struggles, she said disappointedly, "I thought you were perfect, and you're really not." I was the older sister that she looked up to and aspired to be like, but why did I have to appear perfect in order to be admired? I passionately believe that we would all be better off if we were more honest and transparent with each other. I would rather know what my sisters were really going through so that I could walk through it with them rather than them feeling like they had to shamefully hide their struggles for fear of judgment. The people I look up to now are those who unapologetically claim all of who they are—the good and the bad—and are working to be better people. This is who I aspire to be: not perfect, but progressing. There is freedom in our testimony; there is liberation in our transparency.

All that I went through was a blessing in disguise because it brought me closer to Christ and made me recognize the need for a Savior in my life. I am so far from perfect, but part of this entire journey has been realizing that I don't want to be. Not only is perfection overrated, but it completely diminishes life to a set of objectives, and that is not what it is at all. Life is about *experiencing* all that it means to be human.

I have developed a deeper level of appreciation for my journey and have grown to love the God that brought me through it all and can now get the glory because of it. I am grateful for every single one of my experiences and the lessons I learned along the way. If I had found God sooner, would I have saved myself from some hurt? Possibly. But it was in those moments that God came in and rescued me. It was in those moments that God would whisper, "Come back to me." It was in those moments of absolute emptiness when God's voice was clearest, and I realized how much I needed Him. As Joseph said to the family that tried to kill him, "As for you, you meant evil against me, but God meant it for good, to bring it about that many people should be kept alive, as they are today" (Genesis 50:20 ESV). Therefore, I can write this book, knowing that it will shatter many people's perceptions of me, and still be joyful. I am free from the need for validation from other people. I don't need anybody to tell me I am good enough because I have a Creator who declared me more than enough before I was born. God still wanted me to come back to Him no matter how dirty and wounded I felt because He knew my real worth was in my identity as His daughter, not in what I did or didn't do. Because I am defined by God's love now, I can openly share my past and pain openly, knowing it does not determine my identity or destiny.

The unboxing is a process of awakening to who we can become and reframe all that has happened in our lives. The process of unboxing allows us to let go of all that is draining us and keeping us from being our most authentic selves. As we come of age, we can very easily become our own oppressors by maintaining the conditioning that we grew up in. We perform in ways that are contrary to how we were created to live. We carry burdens of shame, insecurity, and fear that we were never meant to carry. We often get so weighed down with life that it is possible to go decades and even all the way to the grave, without ever experiencing the joy that God intended for us before He brought us into this world. The conditioning that we experience is subtle––it doesn't always feel oppressive; sometimes, it feels "normal," or even good. We don't consciously challenge it because it starts when we are young, and it often seems harmless. But as we grow, we can begin to feel the limitations of these walls. If we are honest with ourselves, something in our core is missing. Everyone wants to be loved, to have a sense of security, identity, and worth—that is largely what it means to be human. Many of us go about trying to get all of this by grabbing onto what *other people* told us and holding on to the defense mechanisms that we hope will keep us from getting hurt.

To be free from this striving, we have to be transformed by God's love, unbox who we are, and live in our most authentic light. We must take everything about us and find not only how it connects but also how each aspect of our lives and our identities are essential to becoming the individuals that we are destined to become. We have to look at the things in our life that are draining us, the things that encompass our walls, what lies inside our box, and even the things that we feel have wounded us and reconcile *all of it*. Who we are and what we've been through are not mistakes. We are at our best when we are authentic to our core. As we evolve as people, we cannot allow ourselves to be imprisoned by limiting identities of our past. With confidence in our *whole selves*, we are capable of doing anything we put our minds to.

We are called to reconcile our own identity, create an eternal foundation, and love others. Everyone's journey is going to be different, unique, challenging, and beautiful. As a Christian, I have grown to understand that love is the living water, or the transformative power, that dissolves the walls of our bondage. It is the human condition to have a limited perspective of the box and to desire acceptance and love. Unfortunately, many of us find it in the wrong places. True acceptance and love can only be found in the person of Jesus Christ. We cannot develop a more accurate perspective without God, because it is His perspective that holds our truest identity. When we first encounter God's love, we can feel overwhelmed by the newness of it all, but He teaches us how to rise above our fears and walk confidently forward. He teaches us how to run our race and win. He will even teach us how to bring the water to other peoples' walls. Each and every one of us has the opportunity to accept God's transcendent love that He offers all of us through Christ Jesus.

None of us will get to heaven by good works. This means that being a "good person" isn't what truly justifies us nor will it get us into Heaven. God's standard for entrance into Heaven is perfection. He sent His son Jesus to live a perfect life and die the sinner's death we deserved so that God the Father is able to see Jesus' perfection when He looks at us. Jesus is our only way to enter Heaven. He is the only pathway to living a truly fulfilled and peaceful life. We enter heaven by way of a relationship, not by anything we can do on our own. We must surrender to Christ so that we can have eternal life, not just after death, but starting here on earth because eternal life begins with knowing God (John 17:3).

To embark on our unboxing journey, we must liberate ourselves by developing an awareness of what has shaped us. As I said at the very beginning of this book, our ability to become the most authentic versions of ourselves is dependent on our courage to deeply reflect on the crucial aspects of ourselves. Until we take charge of our lives in this way, we will continue to lay victim to the ever-changing waves of culture around us. Even at ages 15, 16, 17, and 18, I believe there is great value in entering this process of unboxing. What makes you, *you*? Why do you want what you want? Are you limiting your potential because of the people that are around you or because of the lies that you tell yourself about your worth? What does it mean for you to be free? What does it mean for us to be free? Reconcile all of who you are, and no matter how hard, how ugly, how daunting it will be, frame it into something beautiful—find your essence.

It's time for us as young people to come out of hiding and forge our own journeys of unboxing. It is time for us to allow everything inside of us—the good and the bad—to be revealed and healed by God so that He might write an unimaginable story of greatness and beauty through our lives. We all have had experiences that have made us feel unlovable—friendships gone wrong, broken childhoods, and people who betrayed us, but our stories don't have to end there. We are truly loved beyond anything we can imagine, and once we step out of our boxes, and into God's boundless love for us, there is truly no limit to all we can do and become. The freedom of unboxing belongs to you, and once you take hold of it, your world (and our world) will truly never be the same.

What's Next?

I'd love to work with you on your journey to
becoming all that God has called you to be.
Learn more about my coaching programs at unapologeticnicole.com
and be sure to follow me on Instagram @unapologeticnicole.

If you are a student, then be sure to follow my non-profit
LUNA Empowered INC. on Instagram @lunaempowered
and subscribe to our newsletter at lunaempowered.org.
We are an organization for students, by students providing
resources for you to thrive emotionally and spiritually.

I've created "My Unboxing: Mental Health and Faith Journals"
just for you so you can walk through your own unboxing journey
on your own. Be sure to get a copy on LUNA's website.

I can't wait to continue this journey with you!

Printed in the United States
by Baker & Taylor Publisher Services